# RANDOM THOUGHTS 2

Jennifer Johnson

# Copyrights

DEPARTMENT OF JUSTICE
FBI ANTI-PIRACY WARNING
FIDELITY
BRAVERY
INTEGRITY
FEDERAL BUREAU OF INVESTIGATION

# Overview

More Crazy and Random Thoughts from a Weird Author

More blog post collections, Poems, Quotes, and crazy random ideas from the racing mind of one author.

# Dedication:

This is dedicated to all my friends, family, and fans who continue to support my work. Thank you for being there. I hope you enjoy this book.

# Contents

# The Randomness Begins.......

## 1.0 Marriage (What are we thinking!)

Love, lust, commitment....ups, downs, arguments.....what makes a marriage last and be fulfilling? Why do some stay together even without love? Why do some just stay for the kids? The union of a man and a woman, recognized by authority or ceremony, is as old as civilization itself and marriage of some kind is found in virtually every society. But throughout the centuries marriage has taken many different forms. Early marriage was borne of ancient societies' need to secure a safe environment in which to breed, handle the granting of property rights, and protect bloodlines. Even in these early times, marriage was much about love and desire as it was social and economic stability. In its roundness, the engagement ring, a custom dating back to the Ancient Rome, is believed to represent eternity and everlasting union. It was once believed a vein or nerve ran directly from the 'ring' finger of the left hand to the heart.

Understanding of marriage contrasted greatly from culture to culture. Some cultures viewed the institution as endogamous (men were required to marry within their own social group, family, clan, or tribe), exogamous (marrying outside the geographical region or social group) or polygamous (allowing men to take more than one bride). Polygamy was formally banned towards the end of the Roman Empire with laws against adultery, fornication and other relationships outside a monogamous lifelong covenant. It was in the 12th century that the Roman Catholic Church formally defined marriage as a sacrament, sanctioned by God. However, while during the sixteenth century people began to re-value marriage as a merely life-long and monogamous covenant between a man and a woman.

## *Dating*

During the Victorian era romantic love became viewed as the primary requirement for marriage and the rituals of courting became even more formal. An interested gentleman could not simply walk up to a young lady and begin a conversation. He had to be formally introduced and only after some time was considered appropriate for a man to speak to a lady or for a couple to be seen together.

Once formally introduced, if a gentleman wished to escort a lady home from a social function he would present his card to her and at the end of the evening the lady would review her options and chose who would be her escort! She would then notify the lucky gentleman by giving him her own card requesting that he escort her home. Almost all courting took place in the girl's home, always under the eye of watchful parents. If the courting progressed, the couple might advance to the front porch. It was also rare for couples to see each other without the presence of a chaperone, and marriage proposals were frequently written. In some areas of the world, arranged marriage, child marriage, and polygamy, may be practiced. The act of marriage usually creates normative or legal obligations between the individuals involved, and any offspring they may produce. In terms of legal recognition, most states and other jurisdictions limit marriage to opposite-sex couples and a diminishing number of these permit polygyny, child marriages, and forced marriages.

Divorce has existed for about as long as marriage. In most societies, the death of one of the partners terminates the marriage, and in monogamous societies this allows the other partner to remarry, though sometimes after a waiting or mourning period. In some societies, a marriage can be annulled, when an authority declares that a marriage never happened. A marriage may also be terminated through divorce. As of 2012, the Philippines and the Vatican City are the only jurisdictions which do not allow divorce. After divorce, one spouse may have to pay alimony. Laws concerning divorce and the ease with which a divorce can be obtained vary widely around the world. After a divorce or an annulment, the people concerned are free to remarry .A statutory right of two married partners to mutually consent to divorce was enacted in western nations in the mid-20th century. In the United States no-fault divorce was first enacted in California in 1969 and the final state to legalize it was New York in 1989. About 45% of marriages in Britain and, according to a 2009 study, 46% of marriages in the U.S. end in divorce.

The ancient Greeks allowed divorce, but even then the person requesting divorce had to submit the request to a magistrate, who would determine whether or not the reasons given were sufficient. In contrast divorce was rare in early Roman culture. Throughout the last thousand years, divorce was generally frowned upon and from the earliest years of the Christian age the only way to dissolve a marriage was by annulment that was granted only by the Church. In 1533 Henry VIII famously broke England's ties with the Catholic Church and changed the face of our nation forever purely because he wanted to divorce Catherine of Aragon and marry Anne Boleyn. Historically, in most cultures, married women had very few rights of their own, being considered, along with the family's children, the property of the husband; as such, they could not own or inherit property, or represent themselves legally. In Europe, the United States, and other places in the world, beginning in the late 19th century and lasting through the 21st century, marriage has undergone gradual legal changes, aimed at improving the rights of the wife. These changes included abolishing the right of husbands to physically discipline their wives, giving wives property rights, liberalizing divorce laws, providing wives with reproductive rights of their own, and requiring a wife's consent when sexual relations occur.

### *The Weird Things We Do*

In many parts of 16th and 17th century Europe and America the concept of 'bundling' was used. This allowed courting couples to share a bed, but fully clothed with a 'bundling board' to separate them. In some parts of 18th Century Europe a biscuit or small loaf of bread was broken over the head of the bride as she came out from the church. Unmarried guests scrambled for the pieces, and they would place them under their pillows to aid their own fortunes in marriage. It is believed that the tradition of having a wedding cake stems from this.

### ***Types of Marriage***

## *Monogamy*

Monogamy is a form of marriage in which an individual has only one spouse during their lifetime or at any one time.

## *Serial Monogamy*

Governments that support monogamy, may allow easy divorce. In a number of Western countries divorce rates approach 50%. Those who remarry do so on average 3 times. Divorce and remarriage can thus result in serial monogamy, i.e. multiple marriages but only one legal spouse at a time. Serial monogamy creates a new kind of relative, the ex-. The ex-wife, for example, remains an active part of her ex-husband's life, as they may be tied together by transfers of resources (alimony, child support), or shared child custody.

Polygamy is a marriage which includes more than two partners. When a man is married to more than one wife at a time, the relationship is called polygyny, and there is no marriage bond between the wives; and when a woman is married to more than one husband at a time, it is called polyandry, and there is no marriage bond between the husbands. If a marriage includes multiple husbands and wives, it can be called group marriage. Polygyny usually grants wives equal status, although the husband may have personal preferences. One type of polygyny is where only one women get the wife right and status, while other women remain legal house mistresses. Although it does not involve multiple formal marriages, the domestic and personal arrangements follow old polygynous patterns. In some societies such as the Loved of South Africa or Sudan, aristocratic women may become female 'husbands.' this female may take a number of polygamous wives. This is not a lesbian relationship, but a means of legitimately expanding a royal lineage by attaching these wives' children to it. Now most countries explicitly prohibit polygyny today.

### *Group Marriage*

Group marriage is in which more than two persons form a family unit, with all the members of the group marriage being considered to be married to all the other members of the group marriage, and all members of the marriage share parental responsibility for any children arising from the marriage. No country legally condones group marriages, neither under the law nor as a common law marriage, but historically it has been practiced by some cultures of Polynesia, Asia, and Papua New Guinea.

### *Child Marriage*

A child marriage is a marriage where one or both spouses are under the age of 18. Child marriage was common throughout history, even up until the 1900s in the United States. In the state of Delaware, the age of consent for marriage was 7 years old. Today it is condemned by international human rights organizations. Child marriages are often arranged between the families of the future bride and groom, sometimes as soon as the girl is born. However, in the late 1800s in England and the United States, women's activists began calling for raised age of consent laws, which was eventually handled in the 1920s, having been raised to 16-18. In many cases, only one marriage-partner is a child, usually the female, due to the importance placed upon female virginity. Causes of child marriage include poverty or religious. This disables the fear of remaining unmarried and inability of women to work for money. Today, child marriages are widespread in parts of the world; being most common in South Asia and sub-Saharan Africa, with more than half of the girls in some countries in those regions being married before 18. In developed countries child marriage is outlawed or restricted.

## *Temporary Marriages*

Several cultures have practiced temporary and conditional marriages. Pre-Islamic Arabs practiced a form of temporary marriage that carries on The Islamic prophet Muhammad sanctioned a temporary marriage which can provide a legitimizing cover for sex workers. The same forms of temporary marriage have been used in Egypt, Lebanon and Iran to make the donation of a human ovary legal for in vitro fertilization; a woman cannot, however, use this kind of marriage to obtain a sperm donation.

## *Common Law Marriage*

In some locations long term relationships may constitute a common-law marriage. This provides the unmarried partners with various rights and responsibilities; and in some countries the laws recognize cohabitation for taxation and social security benefits.

## *The Incest Taboo*

Societies have often placed restrictions on marriage to relatives, though the degree of prohibited relationship varies widely. Marriages between parents and children, or between full siblings, have been considered incest and forbidden. However, marriages between more distant relatives have been much more common, with one estimate being that 80% of all marriages in history have been between second cousins or closer. Another kind of marriage selection is the levirate marriage in which widows are obligated to marry their husband's brother, mostly found in societies where kinship is based on clan groups.

## *Forced Marriage*

A forced marriage is a marriage in which one or both of the parties is married against their will. Forced marriages continue to be practiced in parts of the world, especially in South Asia and Africa. The customs of bride price and dowry, which exist in parts of the world, can lead to buying and selling people into marriage. Marriage laws refer to the legal requirements which determine the validity of a marriage, which vary considerably between countries.

## *Marriage Restrictions*

Marriage is an institution that is historically filled with restrictions. From age, race, social status, to gender, restrictions are placed on marriage by society for reasons of benefiting the children, passing on healthy genes, maintaining cultural values. Almost all cultures that recognize marriage also recognize to prohibit incest and eugenic reasons, marriage laws have set restrictions for relatives to marry. Direct blood relatives are usually prohibited to marry, while for branch line relatives, laws are wary.

## *Marriage of Convenience*

Sometimes people marry to take advantage of a certain situation, sometimes called sham marriage. For example, green card marriages, every year over 450,000 United States citizens marry foreign-born individuals and petition for them to obtain a Green Card in the United States. Another example would be to save money on health insurance or to enter a health plan with preexisting conditions offered by the new spouse's employer.

---

### *Marriage and Sexual Violence*

---

An issue that is a serious concern regarding marriage and which has been the object of international scrutiny is that of sexual violence within marriage. Throughout much of the history, in most cultures, sex in marriage was considered a ‘right’ that could be taken by force if 'denied'. As the concept of human rights started to develop in the 20th century this has become punishable by law. However due to religious views and tradition and even if the countries has adequate laws against rape in marriage these laws are rarely enforced. For example in Morocco, unmarried girls and women who are raped are often forced by their families to marry their rapist. Because being the victim of rape and losing virginity carry extreme social stigma, and the victims are deemed to have their reputation tarnished, a marriage with the rapist is arranged. This is claimed to be in the advantage of both the victim – who does not remain unmarried and doesn't lose social status – and of the rapist, who avoids punishment. In 2012, after a Moroccan 16-year-old girl committed suicide after having been forced by her family to marry her rapist and enduring further abuse by the rapist after they married.

---

*Marriage and Health*

---

Marriage, like other close relationships, exerts considerable influence on health. Married people experience lower morbidity and mortality across such diverse health threats as cancer, heart attacks, and surgery. Research on marriage and health is part of the broader study of the benefits of social relationships. Social ties provide people with a sense of identity, purpose, belonging and support. Simply being married, as well as the quality of one's marriage, has been linked to diverse measures of health. The health effect of marriage is stronger for men than women. Although people with infectious diseases such as AIDS may now marry, marriage is still illegal for the mentally ill.

## 2.0 Nuclear Warfare

*History and Overview*

Nuclear warfare is a military conflict or political strategy in which nuclear weaponry is used to inflict damage on the enemy. Compared to conventional warfare, nuclear warfare can be vastly more destructive in range and extent of damage. A major nuclear exchange would have long-term effects, primarily from the fallout released, and could also lead to a nuclear winter that could last for decades, centuries, or even millennia after the initial attack. Some analysts claim that with this potential nuclear winter side-effect of a nuclear war almost every human on Earth could starve to death.

Only two nuclear weapons have been used in the course of warfare near the end of World War II. For six months before the atomic bombings, the United States intensely firebombed 67 Japanese cities. Together with the United Kingdom and the Republic of China, the United States called for the unconditional surrender of Japan. The Japanese government ignored this ultimatum. By executive order of President Harry S. Truman, the U.S. employed the uranium-type nuclear weapon code named "Little Boy" on the city of Hiroshima on August 6, 1945, followed three days later by the detonation of the plutonium-type weapon code named "Fat Man" over the city of Nagasaki on August 9. During the following four months, the people who died on the day of the detonation of Hiroshima and Nagasaki, large numbers died from the chronic effects of burns, radiation sickness, and other injuries, compounded by illnesses. The bomb and the effects killed 90,000 to 166,000 people in Hiroshima and 60,000 to 80,000 in Nagasaki. In both cities, most of the dead were civilians.

After World War II, nuclear weapons were also developed by the Soviet Union, the United Kingdom, France , and the People's Republic of China , which contributed to the state of conflict and extreme tension that became known as the Cold War. In 1974, India, and in 1998, Pakistan, two countries that were openly hostile toward each other, developed nuclear weapons. Israel and North Korea are also thought to have developed stocks of nuclear weapons, but their governments have never admitted to having nuclear weapons. South Africa also manufactured several complete nuclear weapons in the 1980s, but subsequently became the first country to voluntarily destroy their domestically made weapons stocks and abandon further production.

After the collapse of the Soviet Union in 1991 and the end of the Cold War, the threat of a major nuclear war between the two nuclear superpowers was thought to have declined. Since then, concern over nuclear weapons has shifted to the prevention of nuclear conflicts and the threat of nuclear terrorism.

### *Prevention vs Development*

Nuclear weapons have been detonated on over two thousand occasions for testing purposes, demonstrations, and development. Some Cold War strategists' state that once a nuclear war took place it would surely render the planet uninhabitable. Even optimistic predictions and theories of the effects of a major nuclear war forecast the death of many millions of victims within a very short period of time. More pessimistic predictions argue that a full-scale nuclear war could potentially bring about the extinction of the human race, or at least it's near extinction, with only a relatively small number of survivors, mainly in remote areas. There would then be a reduced quality of life and life expectancy for centuries afterward.

A study presented at a meeting of the American Geophysical Union in December 2006 asserted that even a small-scale regional nuclear war could produce as many direct fatalities as all of World War II and disrupt the global climate for a decade or more. Even in a regional nuclear conflict scenario in which two opposing nations each used 50 Hiroshima-sized nuclear weapons on major population centers, the researchers predicted fatalities ranging from 2.6 million to 16.7 million per country. Also, they estimated that as much as five million tons of soot could be released, producing a cooling of several degrees over large areas of North America and Eurasia. This would impact most of the grain-growing regions. The cooling would last for years and could be catastrophic.

There have even been concerns presented regarding an accidental nuclear war, in which the use of nuclear weapons is triggered unintentionally. Triggers for this scenario have included malfunctioning early warning devices, targeting computers, deliberate malfeasance by rogue military commanders, consequences of an accidental straying of warplanes into enemy airspace, reactions to unannounced missile tests during tense diplomatic periods, reactions to military exercises, and mistranslated or miscommunicated messages. A number of these scenarios actually occurred during the Cold War, though none resulted in the use of nuclear weapons. Many incidents happened in the United States, due to failed computer chips, misidentifications of large flights of geese, test programs, and failures to notify early warning military personnel of legitimate launches of testing devices, or weather missiles. Despite fears of nuclear effects and the warnings from scientists the development and testing continued.

The two atomic bombings led to post-war Japan's adopting of the Three Non-Nuclear Principles, which forbade the nation from developing nuclear arms, but for several years after World War II, the United States maintained a strategic secret force. B-36 bombers that would be able to attack any potential enemy from bomber bases in the United States. It deployed atomic bombs around the world for potential use in conflicts. Over a period of a few years, many in the American defense community became increasingly convinced of the invincibility of the United States to a nuclear attack. Many proposals were suggested to put all American nuclear weapons under international control as an effort to deter both their usage and an arms race. However, no terms could be arrived at that would be agreed upon. Within the United States the authority to produce and develop nuclear weapons was removed from military control and put instead under the civilian control of the Commission. However, the Soviet Union pursued its own atomic capabilities through a combination of scientific research and espionage. The Soviets had conducted significant nuclear espionage of the project from spies at Los

Alamos, the most significant of which was done by the theoretical physicist Klaus Fuchs. The first Soviet bomb was more or less a deliberate copy of the Fat Man plutonium device.

### *Secret Development Races*

With the nuclear technology broken, worldwide nuclear stealing and planning accelerated. The United Kingdom tested its first independent atomic bomb in 1952, followed by France in 1960 and then China in 1964. While much smaller than the arsenals of the United States and the Soviet Union, Western Europe's nuclear reserves were nevertheless a significant factor in strategic planning during the Cold War. Now each country was racing to be the most powerful in case of war.

The widespread introduction of jet-powered interceptor aircraft upset the war balance. This reduced the effectiveness of the American bomber fleet. In 1949 The United States instituted a program to update the bomber fleet to all jets. The Soviet Union conducted large scale military exercises to explore the possibility of defensive and offensive warfare during a nuclear war. The exercise, under the code name of "Snowball", involved the detonation of a nuclear bomb about twice as powerful as that which fell on Nagasaki and an army of approximately 45,000 soldiers on maneuvers through the center immediately after the blast. The exercise was conducted in 1954.

A revolution in nuclear strategic thought occurred with the introduction of the ballistic missiles in which the Soviet Union first successfully tested in August 1957. The US military gave missile development programs the highest national priority, and several spy aircraft and reconnaissance satellites were designed and deployed to observe Soviet progress.

During the Cold War, the Soviet Union invested in extensive protected civilian infrastructure, such as large bunkers and non-perishable food stores. Civil defense programs were instituted in the United States starting in the 1950s, where schools and other public buildings had basements stocked with non-perishable food supplies, canned water, first aid, and dosimeter and Geiger counter radiation measuring devices. The occasional backyard fallout shelter was built by private individuals.

According to the 1980 United Nations report General and Complete Disarmament: Comprehensive Study on Nuclear Weapons: Report of the Secretary-General, it was estimated that there were a total of about 40,000 nuclear warheads in existence at that time, with a potential combined explosive yield of approximately 13,000 megatons. By comparison, when the volcano Mount Tambora erupted in 1815 - turning 1816 into the Year Without A Summer due to the levels of global dimming sulfate aerosols and ash expelled - it exploded with a force of roughly 1,000 megatons, however it must be noted that comparisons with super volcanos are more misleading than helpful due to the different aerosols released, the likely air burst fusing height of nuclear weapons and the globally scattered location of these potential nuclear detonations all being in contrast to the singular and subterranean nature of a super volcanic eruption. Nonetheless, many people believe that a full-scale nuclear war would result in the extinction of the human species.

Recent studies undertaken by the CIA cite the India-Pakistan conflict as the most likely to escalate into a nuclear war. During the Kargil War in 1999, Pakistan came close to using its nuclear weapons in case the conventional military situation underwent further deterioration. Pakistan's foreign minister had even warned that it would "use any weapon in our arsenal", hinting at a nuclear strike against India. This conflict remains the only war between two declared nuclear powers. The  standoff stoked fears of nuclear war between two countries. Despite these very serious and relatively recent threats, relations between India and Pakistan have been improving somewhat over the last few years. However, with the November 26, 2008 terror attacks, India currently will not rule out war with Pakistan.

Israel is thought to possess somewhere between one hundred and four hundred nuclear warheads. It has been asserted that the submarines which Israel received from Germany have been adapted to carry missiles with nuclear warheads, so as to give Israel a second strike capability. Israel has been involved in wars with its neighbors in the Middle East on numerous occasions. The country's small geographic size and population could mean that the Israeli military might have very little time to react to an invasion or other major threat and could escalate to nuclear warfare very quickly.

Iran appears to be in the process of developing a nuclear weapons, which has greatly heightened fears of a nuclear conflict and arms races. Nuclear terrorism by non-state organizations or individuals is a largely unknown and understudied factor in nuclear deterrence thinking, as states possessing nuclear weapons are susceptible to retaliation. The collapse of the Soviet Union has given rise to the possibility that former Soviet nuclear weapons might become available on the black market .While no warheads are known to have been on the black market, it has been alleged that at least some very small or suitcase-size bombs might be unaccounted for.

This is highly dependent on factors such as if one is indoors or out, the size of the explosion, the proximity to the explosion, and to a lesser degree the direction of the wind carrying fallout. Death is highly likely and radiation poisoning is almost certain if one is caught in the open with no terrain or building masking effects.

However to highlight the variability in the real world, and the effect that being indoors can make, despite the lethal radiation and blast zone extending well past her position at Hiroshima, Akiko Takakura survived the effects of an atomic bomb with only minor injuries, due mainly to her position in the lobby of the Bank of Japan, a reinforced concrete building. In contrast, the unknown person sitting outside, fully exposed, on the steps of the Sumitomo Bank, next door to the Bank of Japan, received lethal third degree burns and was then likely killed by the blast, in that order, within two seconds.

The predictions of the effects of a major nuclear exchange include millions of city dweller deaths within a short period of time. Some predictions argue that a full-scale nuclear war could eventually bring about the extinction of the human race. A number of publications advocate preparations that can allegedly be taken in order to allow the majority of civilians to survive even a total nuclear war. Among the most famous of these is the aptly named Nuclear War Survival Skills.

To avoid injury and death from a nuclear weapons heat flash and blast effects, the two most far ranging prompt effects of nuclear weapons, schoolchildren were taught to duck and cover by an early cold war film . Such advice is once again being given in case of nuclear terrorist attacks. Prussian blue, or Radiogardase, is stockpiled in the US, along with potassium iodide and DPTA as pharmaceuticals useful in treating internal exposure to harmful radioisotopes in fallout. These supplies, however, are only stored near major cities. Publications have also emerged on adapting to a changing diet and supplying nutritional food sources following a nuclear war, with particular focus on agricultural radioecology. Many countries maintain plans for  government continuity following a nuclear attack or similar disasters. In, my opinion a government won't matter after such an event. Most individuals would most likely resort to self-reliance and lack of trust as those who did survive would not be kind to other survivors. I truly believe in such an event it would be to each their own and humans taking on a survival mode mentality.

A number of other countries around the world have taken significant efforts to maximize their survival prospects in the event of large disasters, both natural and manmade. For example, metro stations in Pyongyang, North Korea, were constructed 360 ft. below ground, and were designed to serve as nuclear shelters in the event of war, with each station entrance built with thick steel blast doors. While examples of privately funded fallout shelters are the in Ontario, Canada, one of the best known privately constructed shelters, with a focus on post-war networking and reconstruction. In Switzerland, the majority of homes have an underground blast and fallout shelter. The country has an overcapacity of such shelters and can accommodate slightly more than the nation's population size.

However, the energy produced by a nuclear explosive is millions of times more powerful per gram and the temperatures reached are briefly in the tens of millions of degrees. Energy from a nuclear explosive is initially released in several forms of penetrating radiation. When there is a surrounding material such as air, rock, or water, this radiation interacts with and rapidly heats it to an equilibrium temperature .This causes vaporization of surrounding material resulting in its rapid expansion. Kinetic energy created by this expansion contributes to the formation of a shockwave. In 1942 there was some initial speculation among the scientists developing the first nuclear weapons that there might be a possibility of igniting the Earth's atmosphere with a large enough nuclear explosion.

Much of the destruction caused by a nuclear explosion is due to blast effects. Most buildings, except reinforced or blast-resistant structures, will suffer moderate damage when subjected to overpressures. Data obtained from the Japanese surveys found that 8 psi was sufficient to destroy all wooden and brick residential structures. This can reasonably be defined as the pressure capable of producing severe damage.

Most of the material damage caused by a nuclear air burst is caused by a combination of the high static overpressures and the blast winds. The long compression of the blast wave weakens structures, which are then torn apart by the blast winds. The compression, vacuum and drag phases together may last several seconds or longer, and exert forces many times greater than the strongest hurricane.

Acting on the human body, the shock waves cause pressure waves through the tissues. These waves mostly damage junctions between bone and muscle. Lungs and the abdominal cavity, which contain air, are particularly injured. The damage causes severe hemorrhaging or air embolisms, either of which can be rapidly fatal. The overpressure will cause to damage lungs. Some eardrums would probably rupture.

Nuclear weapons emit large amounts of thermal radiation as visible, infrared, and ultraviolet light, to which the atmosphere is largely transparent. This is known as "Flash". The chief hazards are burns and eye injuries. On clear days, these injuries can occur well beyond blast ranges. Fires may also be started by the initial thermal radiation, but the following high winds due to the blast wave may put out almost all such fires, unless the yield is very high, where the range of thermal effects vastly out ranges blast effects, like that observed in the multi-megaton range. This is because the intensity of the blast effects drops off with the third power of distance from the explosion, while the intensity of radiation effects drops off with the second power of distance. This results in the range of thermal effects increasing markedly more than blast range as higher and higher device yields are detonated. Thermal radiation accounts for between 35-45% of the energy released in the explosion, depending on the yield of the device. However, in urban areas, the extinguishing of fires ignited by thermal radiation may matter little, as in a surprise attack fires may also be started by blast-effect-induced electrical shorts, gas pilot lights, overturned stoves, and other ignition sources, as was the case in the breakfast-time bombing of Hiroshima.

Whether or not these secondary fires will in turn themselves be snuffed out as modern noncombustible brick and concrete buildings collapse in on themselves from the same blast wave is uncertain, not least of which, because of the masking effect of modern city landscapes on thermal and blast transmission are continually examined. When combustible frame buildings were blown down in Hiroshima and Nagasaki, they did not burn as rapidly as they would have done had they remained standing. Moreover, the noncombustible debris produced by the blast frequently covered and prevented the burning of combustible material. Fire experts suggest that unlike Hiroshima, due to the nature of modern U.S. city design and construction, a firestorm in modern times is unlikely after a nuclear detonation. This does not exclude fires from being started, but means that these fires will not form into a firestorm, due largely to the differences between modern building materials. Never the less, survival will be of the fittest. (Or luckiest).

## 3.0 Deathbed Regrets

### I wish I had..........

When it is your time to pass what will be your biggest regrets? Here are the top regrets most nurses have reported their dying patients saying they wish they had done differently.

*Following my dreams*

This was the most common regret of all. When people realize that their life is almost over and look back clearly on it, it is easy to see how many dreams have gone unfulfilled. It is very important to try and achieve at least some of your dreams along the way. Such as choosing the practical job over the one I really wanted or not getting that degree.

*I wish I didn't work so hard.*

Working so much at the expense of family and friendships. They missed their children's youth and their partner's companionship. By simplifying your lifestyle and making conscious choices along the way, it is possible to not need the income that you think you do. How do you balance meeting that short-term deadline at work and sitting down for dinner with your family? It's tough and there are always worries. What will my boss and co-workers think? It's not a big deal if I stay late this one time. I'll make it up with the family this weekend. But the making up never seems to happen. Days turn to months and then years and then decades. And by creating more space in your life, you become happier and more open to new opportunities, ones more suited to your new lifestyle.

*I wish I'd had the courage to express my feelings.*

This one is scary and many people avoid it. They suppressed their feelings in order to keep peace with others. As a result, they settled never became who they were truly wanted to become. Many developed bitterness and resentment they carried as a result. We cannot control the reactions of others. However, although people may initially react when you change the way you are by speaking honestly, in the end it raises the relationship to a whole new and healthier level or it releases the unhealthy relationship from your life. Either way, you win. The changes may be scary, but you only live once; so why not live it to its' fullest potential.

*I wish I had stayed in touch with my friends.*

Often they would not truly realize the full benefits of old friends until their dying weeks. Many had become so caught up in their own lives that they had let friendships slip by over the years. It is common for anyone in a busy lifestyle to let friendships slip. There's usually one childhood or high school friend who we were best buddies with. We might have stayed in touch at first but then got busy. Sometimes, we thought to pick up the phone, but maybe we don't have their number or email any more. We always wonder what it would be like to sit down with them again. It is all comes down to love and relationships in the end.

*I wish that I had let myself be happier.*

Many did not realize until the end that happiness is a choice. That they could have been happier more. Not taken life so seriously. Seems strange to say, but most of us don't know how to have fun. We're way too serious. We don't find the humor in life. We don't joke around. We don't think we're funny. So, we go through life very serious. They had stayed stuck in old patterns and habits. We often get stuck in a comfort zone. Fear of change had them pretending to others, and to their selves, that they were content. When deep within, they longed to laugh properly and have silliness in their life again. We worried about what others thought about us too much. Most of us place way too much importance on what other people around us think about us. In the moment, we think their opinions are crucial to our future success and happiness. On our death beds, none of that matters. They let the responsibilities of life take over and didn't take time out for enjoyment and fun. In the end the feel resentment and bitterness.

*Love*

Romance is a big area of regret for most of us. Maybe we dumped someone that we wish we hadn't. Maybe they dumped us. More people will divorce than stay together. If you ask these folks, they'll tell you that it was for the best. They couldn't take it anymore. And, of course, there are some marriages that shouldn't go on and where divorce is the best for all parties involved. However, if you talk to many people privately, they'll tell you they regret their marriage breaking up. Most play a never-ending game of what might have been for the rest of their lives. It is tough to simply be happy with the love that you've found and takes away from the special moments you have today, if you're constantly thinking back to what you once had. The regrets most of us have is that we didn't correct some or most of those little things along the way. We can't control our spouse but we can control our actions and we know – deep down; we could have done more

### *Traveled*

We wish we had gone on more trips or adventures. Many people and families stay close to home. They don't travel all that much or even vacation at all. Whether it be because they don't have the time or they don't have the money. Yet, big trips with friends and family to Disney World, to another state, or even to the lake are the stuff that memories are made of later in life.

### *Our Children*

Taught my kids to do stuff more and spending more time with the kids. Kids love their parents, but they love doing stuff with their parents even more. And it doesn't have to be a vacation at the Four Seasons. It could be raking leaves, learning how to throw a football, or cleaning up a play room together. We learned all the little habits that we take for granted in our own behavior from mimicking our parents. If we're not making the time to do stuff with our kids, we're robbing them of the chance to mimic us. When we get so busy at work, we comfort ourselves knowing that we're going to stay late at the office again with the idea that we'll make it up by taking our son to a ballgame on the weekend. As long as I spend some quality time with him, we think, it will all balance out. It probably won't. Kids do remember that.

### *Saying or doing what we needed to*

Burying the hatchet with a family member or old friend. I know family members that haven't talked for years. Now, neither one will make a move to improve things because they think they've tried and the other one is too stubborn. They think they've done all they can and washed their hands of the relationship. They'll regret that when one of them is no longer around. Or even perhaps not having the courage to get up and talk at a funeral or important event. When you're close to death, you're probably going to wish you'd gotten over those fears on at least a few occasions, but especially at a loved one's funeral or some important event like a wedding. You are going to wish you had said what you needed to them while they were alive as well.

Not taking care of my health when I had the chance. Everyone doesn't think of their health until there's a problem. And at that point, we promise ourselves if we get better we'll do a better job with our health. It shouldn't take a major issue to get us to prioritize our health and diet. Small habits every day make a big difference here over time.

We can all relate to most of these regrets. We can't change the past, so this list isn't meant for you to start a pity party.

## 4.0 Sudden Unexpected Death Syndrome

Sudden unexpected death syndrome or (SUNDS) is the sudden unexpected death of adolescents and adults, often during sleep. Sudden unexplained death syndrome was first noted in 1977 among Hmong refugees in the US. The disease was again noted in Singapore, when a survey of records showed that 230 otherwise healthy Thai men died suddenly of unexplained causes between 1982 and

1990. In the Philippines, SUNDS affects 43 people per 100,000 people per year. Most of the victims are young males.

SUNDS has been cloaked in superstition. Many Filipinos believe ingesting high levels of carbohydrates just before sleeping was the cause. It has only been recently that the scientific world has begun to understand this syndrome. Victims have not been found to have any organic heart diseases or structural heart problems. However, cardiac activity during SUNDS episodes indicates irregular heart rhythms and ventricular fibrillation. The victim survives this episode if the heart's rhythm goes back to normal. Older Filipinos recommend wiggling the big toe of people experiencing this to encourage their heart to snap back to normal. In the Philippines the cause of occurrence is depicted due to a mythological creature. This hag-like creature sits on the victim's face or chest so as to immobilize and suffocate him.

In Thailand and Laos, the condition appears to affect primarily young men and the only proven way to prevent death is by implantation of a cardioverter defibrillator. However, this phenomenon is well known among the Hmong people who ascribe these deaths to a malign spirit said to take the form of a jealous woman. Some men may even go to sleep dressed as women so as to avoid the attentions of this spirit.

---

*Reality and Science*

---

Sudden death syndrome describes a sudden, unexpected death which may occur during sleep, while awake, or just after exercise. Most deaths are due to a heart condition and are known as sudden arrhythmia death or sudden cardiac death syndrome. Sudden arrhythmia death is most commonly due to a serious abnormal change to the heart's rhythm known as an arrhythmia. Sudden cardiac death describes a sudden death as a result of an un-resuscitated cardiac arrest or heart attack. The majority of sudden deaths are due to inherited heart conditions. Screening family members where there has been a heart condition or a previous sudden death, including a sudden infant death (SIDS), could identify pre-existing conditions that may cause sudden death. Appropriate treatment could then prevent or reduce the risk of sudden death occurring.

There are a number of heart conditions that can cause sudden death syndrome however the cause of sudden death often remains unknown until a post-mortem has been performed. The majority of victims have no warning signs or prior symptoms.

The British Heart Foundation said a study showed that the number of adults who collapse and die suddenly without explanation could be much greater than what was recorded in official statistics. The study examined the frequency of sudden unexpected cardiac or unexplained death in a sample of cases investigated by coroners in England during the 1990s. The study included white people aged 16 to 64 years who had no history of cardiac disease on whom autopsy found either a cardiac or no identifiable cause of death. Most of the 692 people investigated died from heart-related causes. But in 4.1 percent of the cases, no cause could be found despite a full post-mortem examination.

Once cot death became officially labeled as the 'sudden infant death syndrome, or SIDS it was possible to collect and collate the relevant data, identify possible causes and take steps to protect infants from such tragedies, resulting in a 70 percent fall in the number of deaths over a period of 10 years. The conducted a new study that estimated that in England, 3,500 apparently healthy adults die suddenly from cardiac or unexplained causes each year. In about 150 of these deaths there was no cause that could be identified.

The department of forensic medicine and science at the University of Glasgow provides a postmortem examination service for regions in Scotland, of which the population is approximately 2.7 million. Almost all cases of suspicious deaths within this region and also a considerable proportion of natural, suicidal, and accidental deaths are examined. Approximately 60% of 1500 to 2000 deaths comprised of sudden unexpected or unexplained deaths. The records of the department have been reviewed for deaths involving epilepsy, intracranial hemorrhage, meningitis, and tumors found during autopsies.

Epilepsy has long been associated with an increased risk of death other than from trauma or drowning. It is now recognized that individuals with epilepsy are at an increased risk of sudden unexplained death However there have been several risk factors for such deaths  that have been identified and include epilepsy, poor seizure control, multiple drug treatment, alcohol abuse, and unwitnessed seizures.

The investigation of these deaths is variable; in some series only a minority of patients had a postmortem examination. In addition, despite a proportion showing abnormalities the brain is often not formally examined by a neuropathologist.

Sudden death may occur as a result of rapid bleeding into any one part or more of the brain. The causes vary depending upon age and location of the brain hemorrhage. Sudden death from ruptured saccular aneurysm. There has been some uncertainty about the frequency with which aneurysms are associated with rapid death. Based on surveys of large numbers of patients who died before or on arriving at a hospital, found that 60% of the patients died immediately after rupture of an aneurysm. During an autopsy, the diagnosis of brain hemorrhages are evident. These days, hemorrhages are seen increasingly in association with drug abuse and possibly binge alcohol drinking. The drugs most commonly associated with this are ecstasy or other amphetamines, and cocaine. Brain tumors and cysts on the brain are also said to account for 8% of the cases.

There are also several cases each year in which the circumstances strongly suggest that trauma was associated with the deaths. Evidence of trauma may be confined to the head. Most severe forms of traumatic brain injury occur after road traffic accidents or falls from a height. There have been documented instances in which death has been delayed by up to 60 minutes after injury however there are cases where death has occurred rapidly.

The role of physical or emotional stress has been seen as a cause when someone dies from a natural disease process shortly after the event and is a not uncommon medical problem. Such deaths most frequently result from these occurrences as a consequence of a rise in blood pressure. To fully establish a link there must be at least a clear l association between the stressful event and death.

Although are sudden unexplained deaths caused by either acute bacterial meningitis or in association with a large bacterial infection. Acute bacterial meningitis is frequently associated with social and economic deprivation, and alcohol abuse, and is classically associated with pneumonia, a compromised immune system, and an absence of the spleen. This diagnosis can be confirmed by the detection of specific fluids found in the blood.

In detective fiction, any doctor can ascertain the time of death with consummate ease and with breathtaking accuracy. In real life, ascertaining the time of death is very much more difficult and, where the expert treads with great caution. Due to the common event of victims that arrive at hospitals and are presumed dead due to an un-dectable heart rate or very shallow breathing many procedures have been put in place before declaring absolute death.

There are the following items:

- A brief inspection and examination of the body to confirm death.
- Confirm that the body is lifeless with no spontaneous movement and no sign of respiratory effort.

- Confirm there is no pulse. The carotid may be a better place to feel than the radial pulse.
- Confirm there is no breathing effort. Look for signs, listen to the chest.
- After five minutes confirm the absence of pulse and respiratory effort as above.

  Whilst waiting, consider the following:

    - If a body has been dead for a matter of hours, then gravity tends to pool blood and a dependent livid results. If this is not in the lowest parts, as expected, the body has been moved.
    - A cherry red color may suggest carbon monoxide poisoning and is seen only post mortem. It can also occur with organophosphate poisoning.
    - It is appropriate to discreetly inspect the body on both sides to ensure that there are no concealed findings which may be relevant to death.
    - It is much better to discover unexpected or unexplained wounds before the undertaker!
    - Use of the ophthalmoscope to inspect the retina. The characteristic sign is called tracking. The usually continuous lines of the retinal vessels are interrupted like a string of sausages.
    - Note the temperature. Is the body still warm or very cold? Low-reading thermometers are used to measure the temperature of the body and, noting the temperature of the environment, this will

help indicate the time of death. Most doctors, even Forensic Physicians (formerly Police Surgeons) do not carry such an instrument. The job of measuring temperature is now done by Scene of Crime Officers (SOCOs).

- Look at the face. Is the face congested or swollen? Petechial hemorrhages suggest asphyxiation. Inspect the neck. Note any unexplained bruises, abrasions or marks.
- Whilst waiting, have a brief inspection/look around the room. Remember the possibility of death from unnatural causes when considering the history, the mode of death and possible causes of death.
- Be careful about moving more than is necessary, both as a mark of respect but also until it is clear that death was from natural causes. Whilst there is a possibility of death from unnatural causes, the room is a potential crime scene.
- The scene may have been radically changed if cardiopulmonary resuscitation (CPR) has been attempted. For example, the body may have been moved off the bed and on to the floor.
- There may be medicine bottles indicating a disease and possibly glyceryl trinitrate (GTN) immediately at hand, suggesting recent use.

- Emptied bottles of pills, suicide notes and emptied bottles of alcohol are also sometimes enlightening.
- Look again at the body.

Doctors also use clues and items for reports as listed below to alleviate labiality for calling a death.

- Rigor mortis and the estimation of the time of death.
- This is affected by ambient temperature (warmer temperature means faster onset), level of glycogen stores (struggling before death means faster onset).
- 0-3 hours: warm and flaccid.
- 3-8 hours: warm and stiff - small joints (fingers, toes, and jaw) first, then large joints, stiffen.
- 8-36 hours: cold and stiff - small joints start to loosen after 18 hours.
- 36+ hours: cold and flaccid.
- Stating an accurate cause of death is important to obtain meaningful epidemiological data to identify health needs and perhaps to uncover hidden risks.
- If there is any doubt or suspicion about the cause of death, then call the police immediately.
- Futile attempts at resuscitation should be curtailed (for example, on a body that is cold or has rigor mortis). However, drowning or near drowning, especially in

a child with hypothermia may well merit very persistent attempts at resuscitation.

- Attempted resuscitation on a patient with a known terminal disease is inappropriate and unkind.
- The younger a person who dies suddenly, the more important it is that the death should be fully investigated. Exertion can cause sudden death with aortic stenosis or cardiomyopathy even in adolescents. Sudden death in young people may also be associated with drug abuse. Sudden infant death syndrome (SIDS) must be fully investigated.
- A coroner's verdict of suicide is distressing to the family and it does appear that an open verdict is often given rather than a verdict of suicide

Researchers hope to identify genes associated with sudden death and discover previously unrecognized genetic causes for these types of cases. The findings will be used to develop preventative screening programs and potentially life-saving interventions. Using state of the art DNA sequencing and powerful analytics tools it is possible determine the root cause of sudden unexpected death in many families. The progress of science.

## 5.0 Curse of Pearl Byran

Pearl Bryan was a 22-year-old pregnant American woman from Greencastle, Indiana who was found decapitated in Fort Thomas, Kentucky in 1896. Her head was severed. Due to the murder's gruesome nature, it achieved significant notoriety at the time. More recently, there have been claims that her ghost haunts Bobby Mackey's Music World located in Wilder, Kentucky. Her body was identified by the tag in her custom made shoes from Greencastle, Indiana.

Pearl Bryan was the twelfth child of a prosperous farmer who lived in the small town of Greencastle, Indiana. By the age of 22 Pearl was considered a catch. When her cousin, William Wood introduced her to a student, Scott Jackson who attended the Ohio College of Dental Surgery in Cincinnati, she fell in love. Scott Jackson was a student but he was much older than Pearl. He came from a prominent family so her folks did not object to his courtship.

Jackson managed to seduce Pearl and she later found herself pregnant and hiding this fact from her family and friends. Jackson upon hearing the news Pearl was pregnant told William to arrange for Pearl to come to Cincinnati to have an abortion. Pearl told her parents that she was going to Indianapolis. She then went to meet his roommate, a man by the name of Alonzo Walling in Cincinnati. Pearl was 5 months pregnant. This would be the last time Pearl's parents would see her alive. Unfortunately for Pearl, Jackson's medical schooling was in dentistry, and he knew little or nothing about how to perform an abortion and ended up only mutilating the girl horribly. Scared and unable to figure out what to do and how to stop the bleeding, Jackson and Walling ended up murdering the girl by severing her head.

Early in the morning of February 1, 1896 seventeen year-old Jack Hewling was walking along an abandoned lane on the Locke farm where he worked in Wilder, Kentucky. He spotted what he thought was a bundle of clothes. He then realized he was looking at the body of a dead woman. Horror overcame him as he saw that just above the shoulders of this corpse was a bloody stump. The head was missing.

Jackson was soon arrested for the murder and later implicated Alonzo Walling. Jackson and Walling were later convicted and hanged in early 1897.

Even after then men were caught they never revealed what they did with the head. They were offered a deal to avoid being executed if they would reveal the head's location, yet they refused and took their secret to their graves. They reportedly were more afraid of Satan's wrath in the afterlife than any mortal threats to their physical bodies. They were the last people hanged in Newport. The gallows located behind the courthouse were torn down following the execution. The actual double-hanging was urged to be done hastily due to the threat of a public lynching by friends and relatives of Bryan. Pearl Bryan's headless body is buried in the family plot at Forest Lawn Cemetery in Greencastle.

# 6.0 Waverly Hills

*The History*

Waverly Hills is a very spooky post tuberculosis hospital in Jefferson County. The land that is today known as Waverly Hill was purchased by Major Thomas H. Hays in 1883 as the Hays' family home. Since the new home was far away from any existing schools, Mr. Hays decided to open a local school for his daughters to attend. He started a one-room schoolhouse on Pages Lane and hired Lizzie Lee Harris as the teacher. Due to Miss Harris' fondness for Walter Scott's Waverley novels, she named the schoolhouse Waverley School. Major Hays liked the peaceful-sounding name, so he named his property Waverley Hill.

In the early part of 1911, the city of Louisville began to make preparations to build a new Louisville City Hospital, and the hospital commissioners decided in their plans that there would be no provision made in the new City Hospital for the admission of pulmonary tuberculosis, and the Board of Tuberculosis Hospital was given $25,000 to erect a hospital for the care of advanced cases of pulmonary tuberculosis.

The Board of Tuberculosis Hospital kept the name when they bought the land and opened the sanatorium as in the early 20th century; Jefferson County was severely stricken with an outbreak of tuberculosis. In1912, all tuberculosis patients from the City Hospital were relocated to temporary quarters in tents on the grounds of Waverly Hills pending the completion of a hospital for advanced cases. To try to contain the disease, a two-story wooden sanatorium was built which consisted of an main building and two open air pavilions, each housing 20 patients, for treatment. Later that year it opened for the treatments.

There were many tuberculosis cases in Louisville at the time because of all the swampland, which was perfect for the tuberculosis bacteria. Because tuberculosis was so extremely contagious and at epidemic proportions, those living with it could not be allowed to live and exist among the general population. It was not known at the time that tuberculosis was an airborne disease.

In 1914 a children's pavilion added another 50 beds making the capacity around 130 patients. The children's pavilion was not only for sick children but also for the children of tuberculosis patients who could not be cared for properly otherwise. This report also mentions that the goal was to add a new building each year to continually grow.

In 1924 Due to constant need for repairs on the wooden structures as well as need for more beds so that people would not be turned away due to lack of space. Construction of a five-story building that could hold more than 400 patients began. The new building opened in 1926. Waverly Hills had grown so large and isolated it had its own post office, water treatment facility, grew its own fruits and vegetables, raised its own meat for slaughter and maintained many of the other necessities of everyday life. Everyone at Waverly including patients, nurses, doctors and other employees had to say goodbye to everything they knew on the outside world. Once you went to Waverly Hills, you became a permanent resident on the hill.

A medical breakthrough in 1944 was the discovery of an antibiotic that successfully treated and cured Tuberculosis. The remaining patients were sent to Hazelwood Sanatorium in Louisville. Waverly Hills closed down and quarantined, then renovated in 1961.It was. In 1962, the building reopened as WoodHaven Medical Services, a geriatric facility. Primarily treating aging patients with various stages of dementia and mobility limits, as well as the severely mentally handicapped. Woodhaven was closed by the state in 1982 allegedly due to patient neglect, as is sometimes common in these environments of under staffed and overcrowded institutions. Rumors later inaccurately termed Woodhaven as an insane asylum lending too many urban legends.

In 1983 a group of developers began to convert the building into a state prison, but the plan fell through. It was only after this that the property went into a cycle of intermittent abandonment and recapitulation. Over the next few decades Waverly Hills would fall into more dark times. Vandalized, damaged, nearly condemned. Previous property owners had no desire to maintain the buildings luster, and did little to stop people from slowly destroying her. It is sad that a place that played such a vital role during this period of history and medical discovery was not only over, but now disrespected. But in 2001 Waverly Hills Sanatorium was purchased by historical and paranormal enthusiasts Charles and Tina Mattingly. Since then, there have been many changes and improvements to the building and surrounding property.

### *Legends and Ghosts*

A local myth about the death of a nurse by murder or suicide in Room 502. Legend says the nurse found out she was pregnant by the owner of the sanatorium without being married and had contracted tuberculosis, so she hanged herself with a light bulb wire outside the room she was in at the time.

### *Then There's the Death Tunnel.*

It's an inclined ramp with an elaborate motorized conveyor that, some say, was used to transport corpses on gurneys out of the building. This Tunnel is famous for being a haunted hot spot for paranormal activity.

Some urban legends claim that 63,000 deaths occurred at the Sanatorium. According to death records the highest number of deaths in a single year at Waverly Hills was 152. The highest record for deaths was at the end of the Second World War when troops were returning from overseas with very advanced tuberculosis cases. Some independent researchers suggest that since 162 people died at Waverly Hills in 1945, the highest total number of deaths possible over 50 years was approximately 8,212.

There are also stories of a homeless man and his dog that died in an elevator shaft and their ghosts can be spotted in their death spot. Another story is of a child who roams the halls on the floor that housed the children's wing. It is said if you place a ball in an area, leave, and return later the ball will be in a different location.

There are reports of lighting showing the wrong direction from where windows are present and breezes flowing where should be none. Most visitors now enjoy areas such as the morgue where they dare each other to lay in the death chambers or the surgical rooms where it has been said hunched over ghosts have been seen. As a cure doctors would perform surgeries to removed ribs for easier breathing thus without this support left patients a hunched over painful mess.

## 7.0 Lyle and Erik Mendez

Joseph Lyle Menendez (born January 10, 1968) and Erik Galen Menendez (born November 27, 1970) are brothers who are known for their conviction in a highly publicized trial for the shotgun murders in 1989 of their parents, Jose and Kitty Menendez, residents of Beverly Hills, California.

---

### *The Parents*

---

Jose was born in 1944 to an upper-middle class family in Havana, Cuba. His father was a well-known soccer player who owned his own accounting firm. His mother was a swimmer who was elected to Cuba's sports hall of fame. Jose had two older sisters, Teresita and Marta. Although the family was not rich, Jose's parents' accomplishments in sports guaranteed them an honored place in Cuban society. Jose was five years younger than Terry and was spoiled and adored by his mother. In 1960,when Jose was 16 years old Castro came to power and Jose's parents saw that their lives in Cuba were forever changed. They decided to leave Cuba. Jose flew to the United States with Terry's fiancé and settled in Pennsylvania. Jose arrived penniless and did not speak or understand English but was determined to succeed in his adopted country. Jose studied diligently in high school and worked part-time to earn spending money. Due to financial hardship, Jose was not able to achieve one of his dreams, which was to attend an Ivy League college. He promised himself that someday, when he had children, they would achieve his dream and graduate from an Ivy League college. Jose won an athletic scholarship in swimming to Southern Illinois University. Jose did not like Southern Illinois University and is remembered by classmates as withdrawn and sullen. Jose supported himself financially with his athletic scholarship, but eventually walked away from athletics to concentrate on his studies. There was one person who made Jose feel good. Her name was Kitty Andersen.

Kitty was born in 1941, the youngest of four children of Charles and Mae Andersen. Her family lived in a suburb south of Chicago. During her early childhood, Kitty's family was solidly middle class. Her father owned a heating and air-conditioning business that did well and her mother stayed at home to care for Kitty and her two older brothers, Milt and Brian, and older sister Joan.

Although the family appeared to be loving, Kitty's father beat her mother in front of their children as well as beat his children. Before Kitty entered grammar school, her father left her mother for another woman. In order to support her family, Kitty's mother worked for United Airlines at Midway Airport outside of Chicago. Kitty's parents eventually divorced. Kitty's father remarried. Her mother never remarried and became bitter and depressed by the divorce. Kitty grew up convinced that divorce was the worst thing that could happen in a woman's life. Kitty hated her father and did not have any contact with him for many years after her parents' divorce. In her senior year of high school, Kitty was accepted by Southern Illinois University. Kitty dreamed that after she graduated from college, she would pursue a career in producing and directing commercial radio and television programs in New York City.

Kitty and Jose met during Kitty's senior year of college and Jose's freshman year of college. After only a short time, Kitty and Jose became inseparable. To Jose, Kitty was attractive not only physically, but in what she represented. Kitty was the daughter of a shopkeeper, the offspring of the American merchant class. By winning Kitty, Jose was establishing his claim to his new country. Jose fulfilled something for Kitty too. Kitty felt that there was a depth to Jose that few people understood or appreciated. She saw someone who was willing to work hard and overcome hardships, not someone who was willing to slide by on family connections or money, like her privileged classmates. Jose told Kitty of his plan to make it big in the business world.

When Jose and Kitty were seen together around the Southern Illinois campus, people would stop and stare. In the early 1960s, people were conservative and people from different ethnic backgrounds did not mix. The civil rights movement in America was centered in the South and had yet to reach Carbondale. Their ages and background differences did not seem to matter to Kitty and Jose; they were determined to spend their lives together. Jose and Kitty's relationship caused problems for both of their families. Jose and Kitty eloped and were secretly married in 1963.

After their marriage, Jose and Kitty moved to New York City. During the early years of her marriage, Kitty's dreams of working in broadcasting began to fade and she discarded her plans to obtain a master's degree, in order to support Jose and his career. Jose graduated from Queen's College with a CPA degree. He went to work for Coopers & Lybrand, an international accounting firm. Kitty continued to teach grade school. After their first son was born Kitty became a stay at home mother. 1971, Jose went to work at Hertz, as an executive in the car leasing division and the Menendez family moved from Illinois to the East Coast and settled in New Jersey. Jose's second son, Erik, was then born. In 1981, Jose was assigned to RCA's record division. In 1981, Kitty also uncovered one of Jose's relationships and walked out of their home for several days. Jose managed to convince her to come home, more so for the brothers than because he loved her. By 1985, at the age of 41, Jose had risen to become the executive vice president and chief operating officer for RCA Records' worldwide operations.

Through contacts that Jose had made while at RCA, he was able to find a position as the President of LIVE Entertainment in California. Jose jumped at the chance to become involved in the film business and had no problem uprooting his family and moving them from the East Coast to the West Coast. Kitty wasn't so positive about the move. She had spent the past 16 years building a life outside of her marriage. Kitty had an established a network of friends who she cared about and who in turn cared about her. Nevertheless, Jose decided that it would be in Kitty and Erik's best interests to move to California with him. They settled in Calabasas, an upper-middle class suburb in the northwestern part of the San Fernando Valley. Lyle remained beyond in Princeton to attend college.

Jose dedicated himself to raising great sons who would carry out his plans for the future and continue his legacy. Because Jose had fought his way up the corporate ladder, he understood that there was an easier and more refined way to reach the top and he set about training his sons to reach that peak. When the brothers were young, Jose had rules for everything: what they could eat, who they could spend time with, and what they read and thought about. Every hour of every day was to be accounted for. Jose and Kitty did not take in to account that they were dealing with young children, nor did they consider that their children could be flawed or that they themselves might be flawed. Jose's greatest flaw was his viciousness that probably grew out of his insecurity about his ethnicity.

The pressures of meeting Jose's demands appeared early on Lyle and Erik. Both brothers developed stutters, stomach pains and had a habit of grinding their teeth. Both brothers also developed nasty tempers. As they grew older, the brothers were drawn to each other for companionship and solidarity in order to face their father's control. Erik's worship of Lyle probably came from the fact that Jose was so remote that his younger son did not feel he could approach him. Lyle was approachable, while Jose was an overwhelming presence.

In 1979, Lyle and Erik attended the Princeton Day School, a private school. At the Princeton Day School both brothers were considered average students. Lyle developed problems academically when he was in the sixth grade. His teacher found that he was not well prepared and did not have the ability to concentrate. Teachers felt that both Lyle and Erik had learning problems, but Jose would not accept that his sons had flaws. The teachers noticed that the homework the brothers turned in was far better than the work completed in class. Teachers also noticed that the brothers were immature compared to their classmates. At the age of 14, Lyle still wet his bed and played with stuffed animals.

There were other signs that the boys were headed for serious trouble. In 1982, when Erik and Lyle were about twelve and fifteen, their cousin stayed with the family for the summer. One night, the three cousins began to playfully wrestle. Suddenly Lyle and Erik began to undress Diane. Without saying a word, the brothers tied her up and stripped off her shirt. Diane screamed and the brothers retreated from their attack. Around the same time, Diane experienced another attack. This time, she and Lyle were watching television. Without warning, Lyle struck. He climbed on top of her and began to fondle her. Like the attack that came earlier, she had not enticed Lyle and the attack ceased as soon as she was able free herself.

From a young age, Lyle and Erik Menendez were attached to each other in a way that seemed abnormal. Dealing with a successful business executive father who enforced rigid rules and expected nothing but the best from his sons may have made them too dependent on each other. The Menendez brothers grew up in Princeton, New Jersey. Both of them attended Princeton Day School for grade school, and Lyle attended Princeton University. After the family moved to California in 1987 when their father got a job at Carolco, Erik attended high school in Calabasas, California. Lyle was placed on academic probation at Princeton for poor grades and disciplinary probation, and he eventually dropped out after allegations of plagiarism.

---

*Lyle*

---

Lyle's first romance came when he was fifteen. His relationship with his girlfriend, Stacey Feldman was innocent and pure. Their first date was to see Raiders of the Lost Ark. Lyle was a huge movie fan and going to the movies was, perhaps, the only experience that Lyle was able to enjoy for himself without having it filtered through his parents. Lyle seemed to have grown up completely believing to be true what he saw on the movie screen. He never seemed to be able to distinguish between fact and fiction. Stacey and Lyle fell in love. They walked around school hand in hand which was against the rules. Teachers and administrators let this infraction pass because they felt that Stacey and Lyle were awkward kids who needed each other. At the end of the school year, Lyle and Stacey were voted "most married" by their classmates. Lyle and Stacey talked about getting married and having children. Lyle lavished jewelry and other gifts on

Stacey. Stacey ended the relationship when she went off to college, realizing that she wanted to experience more of life and that she was too young to get married. Lyle was hurt by Stacey's rejection and tried to win her back by promising to buy her a fur coat. Stacey was not interested and Lyle moved on.

Jose dreamed that Lyle would attend an Ivy League college. Lyle, who was not a good student, told his friends that he wanted to skip college and open a restaurant with his father's financial backing. Jose would not entertain thoughts of anything less than an Ivy League education for Lyle. When Lyle initially applied to Princeton he was rejected. He enrolled in a local community college and submitted another application to Princeton for another school year. While Lyle waited to hear from Princeton, he met and began to date Jaime. Jaime was also a tennis player and five years older than Lyle was. Kitty and Jose did not like Jaime because they felt that Jaime was dating Lyle because he was the son of wealthy parents.

Lyle was accepted to Princeton more on the strength of his ethnicity and ability to play tennis, than on his standardized test scores and high school grades that were just average. During the summer of 1987, Lyle and Jaime announced that they were engaged. This announcement angered Jose. At 19, Jose felt that Lyle was too young to be married. Shortly before Lyle was to begin at Princeton, Jaime moved to Alabama to teach tennis and Lyle followed her. Jose was upset by this and secretly arranged to sponsor Jaime on a European tennis tour. Jose thought that once Jaime was out of the picture, Lyle could concentrate on Princeton without any distractions. Jose was wrong. Lyle followed Jaime to Europe.

During his first semester at Princeton, Lyle was accused of plagiarism. During this time, Lyle was traveling back and forth on weekends to California to visit his family. During the weekend before this psychology lab was due, Lyle had traveled to California and lost his notebook with his notes in the airport. Lyle asked his lab partner if he could look at his assignment. The assignment that Lyle handed in resembled Lyle's lab partners so closely that the instructor singled it out and brought it to the attention of campus authorities. Lyle hated school and rarely participated in campus activities. He was so devoted to winning and being first that he had a difficult time just being one of many struggling students competing at an Ivy League college. Although Lyle was humiliated and wanted to transfer to UCLA, or the University of Pennsylvania, Jose would not hear of it.

During the year that Lyle was out of school, Jose made sure that he was kept busy. Jose was concerned that he was giving his sons too many advantages and creating rich spoiled brats. Jose put Lyle to work at LIVE. Lyle was responsible for reviewing expense reports and looking for ways to improve efficiency and reduce costs. Lyle was treated like any other employee and had to make an appointment to see Jose.

When Lyle returned to Princeton in the fall of 1988, he continued his relationship with Jaime Pisarcik. Lyle's return to Princeton began badly when he discovered that he was assigned a roommate. Lyle wanted a single. According to the hall's student advisor, when Lyle saw the belongings of the other student in the room, he threw them in the hall. Jose came to Lyle's defense. He wrote a letter to Princeton requesting a single for Lyle. Lyle was given a single and like the previous year, did not participate in any campus activities

During the spring of 1989, Lyle began to date a model named Christy. Christy was 30 years old, nine years older than Lyle was. This relationship upset both Jose and Kitty. There was another issue that upset Jose even more and that was Lyle's continued desire to transfer to UCLA. Lyle was tired of Princeton, but Jose would not entertain any thoughts of Lyle transferring to another school. Lyle's girlfriend Christy told him that she was pregnant. Jose found out and went to see her. According to Lyle, Jose intimidated her into having an abortion. Kitty later told one of her friends that Jose paid Christy $100,000. After paying Christy off, Jose and Kitty demanded that Lyle give her up for good.

---

*Erik*

---

Erik grew up emulating his older brother and for a time lived in the shadow of Lyle, especially at the Princeton Day School. It seemed that neither brother fit in at school. They were both considered mysterious loners, who laughed only at their own private jokes. They did not join in or play with other children. Erik's schoolwork, like Lyle's, was average. Throughout grade and high school, Kitty completed much of Erik's homework for him. Erik learned early in life that Jose was grooming Lyle to become the future leader of the family. He grew up sad and withdrawn.

When Jose, Kitty and Erik moved to California in 1986, Erik was a sophomore in high school. Erik enrolled at Calabasas High School. Away from his brother and the comparisons that were often made between them at the Princeton Day School, Erik found his own identity. Erik made friends with a group of boys who were like him, cocky, loud and with a rebellious streak.

Kitty had been worried about Erik's sexual orientation for some time. Kitty believed that Erik was homosexual. When they moved to Calabasas, Kitty gave Erik an order to find a girlfriend in six months. Erik found an older girl at Calabasas High, but their relationship was short lived. At a party, Erik and the girl argued and Erik locked the girl in a room. He would not let her leave. She screamed and yelled, but Erik would not let her out. Finally, Erik let the girl go. The girl had enough of Erik. Erik later had another girlfriend, Janice, whom Kitty and Jose both liked. Unlike Lyle's girlfriends whom Kitty found cheap, Kitty thought highly of Janice.

Perhaps Erik's most important relationship at Calabasas High was with Craig Cignarelli. Craig was the captain of the tennis team and Erik was the number one-ranked player on the team. Craig and Erik spent a great deal of time together and wrote a third rate screenplay entitled Friends. The script was a sixty-two-page thriller about a son from a wealthy family who reads his parents' will and learns that upon their deaths, he will inherit $157 million. The son murders everyone to get his hands on his parents' money before being killed.

### *Together*

In July 1988, Erik and Lyle began breaking into homes in Calabasas. The brothers burglarized the homes owned by parents of their friends and were surprised by the large amounts of cash and jewelry that they were able to steal. The brothers had found an easy source of spending money, rather than having to ask Jose for a hand out, or listen Jose lecture about hard work.

The amount of money and jewelry that Lyle and Erik stole was estimated to be more than $100,000, large enough to be classified as a felony offense called grand theft burglary. The Los Angeles County sheriff's detective who investigated the burglaries received a break in the case after Erik was stopped for a driving violation in Calabasas and stolen property was found in his car trunk. Later the detective discovered that a safe in one of the homes that the brothers had burglarized was found in another home burglarized by the brothers. It appeared that the thieves had developed a guilty conscience and returned a safe they had stolen to the wrong home.

Jose was furious about the burglaries. Jose did not want his sons to spend any time in jail and hired a well-respected criminal defense attorney to represent them. The defense attorney was able to work out an agreement with the district attorney's office that would absolve Lyle of any participation in the burglaries, if

Erik took responsibility for all the crimes. A judge to sentence Erik to community service with the homeless and for the brothers to undergo psychological counseling. Jose wrote a check for $11,000 to the victims to cover items that had been stolen by the brothers, but that had disappeared and could not be returned.

Jose and Kitty could not understand what was wrong with their sons. There were so many problems with Lyle and Erik. Jose was losing his patience and was less and less willing to be persuaded by Lyle's rationalizations. Jose and Kitty were so desperate to drive home to their sons how serious their circumstances were that they used the only thing that they thought would get through to them; they threatened to rewrite their wills and leave the brothers out completely.

As the summer came to an end, tensions in the house seemed to escalate. Kitty began to lock the door to her bedroom at night and she kept two twenty-two rifles in her closet. She would not allow Lyle and Erik to have keys to the house. When the brothers came home at night, Kitty would let them into the house, even if she had to be awakened from sleep. It was apparent that something was frightening Kitty.

They committed home burglaries together, did poorly in school and avoided contact with others. Their mother, Kitty, reeling from her husband's infidelity and both her sons' diagnosed sociopathic tendencies, kept a close eye on Lyle, 21, a Princeton student, and Erik, 18, who was UCLA bound. But not the kind of watchful eye that parents usually have; this was a woman who feared for her safety. , Kitty went to her therapist and told him that she feared her sons were sociopaths.

After watching a TV miniseries, based on real life events, told the story of a group of young men from Beverly Hills who planned and carried out two murders, they began to discuss killing their father. Each brother complained to the other about how domineering and controlling their father was, how impossible it was for either brother to please him, how he planned to disinherit both brothers from his will and how poorly he treated their mother. The brothers rationalized that if they killed their father, they would have to kill their mother because she could not survive emotionally without their father. She could also be a living witness to the crime they were about to commit.

Lyle and Erik eventually decided they would rid themselves of their abusive father and save their mother the anguish of living without him by killing her too. They shot their parents to death at their Beverly Hills mansion in early 1989.

Jose and Kitty were tired that summer evening because the family had been out shark fishing on a chartered yacht, Motion Picture Marine, until midnight the previous day. The neighbors reported hearing what sounded like firecrackers, but dismissed it as nothing to be concerned about. Jose was shot point-blank in the back of the head with a Mossberg 12-gauge shotgun. Kitty made a run for the hallway but was shot in the leg, causing it to break. She was shot several times in the arm, chest, and face, leaving her unrecognizable. Both of them were then shot in the kneecap to make the crime appear mob related. The brothers then left and dumped their shotguns. They bought tickets at a local movie theater to use as an alibi. When the brothers returned home, Lyle called

911. The police immediately considered the brothers suspects, but had no leads.

Kitty was agitated in the time leading up to the murders, constantly locking her bedroom door at night and keeping a rifle in her wardrobe for safekeeping. It was clear that something was troubling her. Kitty did mention to her psychiatrist, a few weeks before the murders, that she was afraid her sons might be sociopaths.

Lyle and Erik staged an elaborate memorial service for Jose and Kitty in August 1989 at the Directors Guild of America in Los Angeles. Lyle and Erik arrived one hour late. Erik looked uncomfortable, and his face was red and swollen. Lyle appeared calm and cool. To Lyle, this event marked his arrival in the business world. Up to this moment, the world had known Lyle through Jose's bragging of his accomplishments on the tennis court and his admission to Princeton. Lyle wanted to prove that he was ready to take his place as the head of the Menendez family and he was determined to assert himself as Jose's legitimate replacement. Later in August of1989, a traditional church service was held at the university chapel in Princeton. At the service, Lyle spoke for thirty minutes and recalled how much Jose and Kitty had meant to him. Erik was too upset to speak.

For seven months after the murders they went on shopping sprees, started fake businesses and lived in hotels paid for by their father's company. By the end of 1989, they had spent more than a million dollars. Police found the spending suspicious, but what actually led to the brothers' arrest was Erik's breakdown and full confession to a psychotherapist. On December 8, 1992, the Menendez brothers were indicted by the Los Angeles County Grand Jury on charges that they had murdered their parents

The Menendez brothers and the murder of their parents became a national sensation when Court TV broadcast the trial in 1993. The younger brother's defense attorney, Leslie Abramson, vaulted to fame with her defense, alleging that the brothers were driven to murder by a lifetime of abuse from their parents, including sexual abuse from their father, Jose. Despite the theory, the past criminal records of the brothers stood in contrast to the theory. The trial ended in two deadlocked juries. Los Angeles District Attorney Gil Garcetti immediately announced that the brothers would be retried.

Both brothers were convicted of two counts of first-degree murder and conspiracy to commit murder. In the penalty phase of the trial, the jury did not support death sentences for the brothers but instead recommended life in prison. The jury stated that the abuse defense was never a factor in their decisions and that the jury rejected the death penalty because neither brother had a felony record or a history of violence. Unlike the previous trials, the jury unanimously rejected the defense theory that the brothers killed their parents out of fear, but believed rather that the murders were committed with the intent of gaining control of their parents' considerable wealth.

In 1996, Lyle and Erik Menendez was sentenced to life in prison without the possibility of parole. Judge Weisberg sentenced the brothers to consecutive sentences for the murders and the charge of conspiracy to commit murder. The Department of Corrections separated the Menendez brothers, sending them to different prisons. Both were classified as maximum-security inmates and were segregated from other prisoners. Since entering prison, both brothers have married, even though California does not allow conjugal visits for those convicted of murder or for those serving life sentences.

In 1997, Lyle married longtime pen pal Anna Eriksson, a former model. The marriage reportedly ended after less than a year after she reportedly discovered that Lyle was cheating on her by writing to another woman. In 2003, Lyle, then married Rebecca Sneed, a 33-year-old magazine editor at a ceremony in a maximum security visiting area. Lyle and Rebecca had reportedly known each other for approximately 10 years prior to their engagement.

In 1997, Erik was reportedly married through a telephone ceremony at Folsom State Prison. In June 1999, Erik, then married Tammi Ruth Saccomanat Folsom State Prison in a prison waiting room. Tammi Menendez also self-published a book in 2005 titled They Said We'd Never Make It - My Life with Erik Menendez, though Erik stated that he had heavily edited the book.

Under the terms of the sentences for their multiple crimes, the brothers are expected to spend the remainder of their lives in prison. According to Erik, he and his brother have not spoken to each other for more than ten years.

## 8.0 Leopold and Loeb

Nathan Freudenthal Leopold, Jr. (November 19, 1904 – August 29, 1971) a brilliant law student, a published ornithologist, and the heir to a manufacturing fortune and Richard Albert Loeb (June 11, 1905 – January 28, 1936), graduate student, was smart, handsome, charming and wealthy were more commonly known as "Leopold and Loeb". They kidnapped and murdered 14-year-old Robert "Bobby" Franks in 1924 in Chicago. The duo was motivated to murder Franks by their desire to commit a perfect crime. They proved sloppy criminals.

Leopold was brilliant. He had an IQ of over 200 and excelled at school. By age 19, Leopold had already graduated from college and was in law school. Leopold was also fascinated with birds and was considered an accomplished ornithologist. However, despite being brilliant, Leopold was very awkward socially.

Richard Loeb was also very intelligent, but not to the same caliber as Leopold. Loeb, who had been pushed and guided by a strict governess, had also been sent to college at a young age. However, once there, Loeb did not excel; instead, he gambled and drank. Unlike Leopold, Loeb was considered very attractive and had impeccable social skills.

## *Early Life*

The two young men grew up with their families in the affluent Kenwood neighborhood on Chicago's South Side. The Loeb's owned a summer estate, Castle Farms, in Charlevoix, Michigan, in addition to their mansion in Kenwood, two blocks from the Leopold home.

Nathan Leopold was brilliant. He had an IQ of over 200 and excelled at school. By age 19, Leopold had already graduated from college and was in law school. Leopold was also fascinated with birds and was considered an accomplished ornithologist.

However, despite being brilliant, Leopold was very awkward socially. Richard Loeb was also very intelligent, but not to the same caliber as Leopold. Loeb, who had been pushed and guided by a strict governess, had also been sent to college at a young age. However, once there, Loeb did not excel; instead, he gambled and drank. Unlike Leopold, Loeb was considered very attractive and had impeccable social skills.

It was at college that Leopold and Loeb became close friends. Their relationship was both stormy and intimate. Leopold was obsessed with the attractive Loeb. Loeb, on the other hand, liked having a loyal companion on his risky adventures. The two teenagers, who had become both friends and lovers, soon began committing small acts of theft, vandalism, and arson. Eventually, the two decided to plan and commit the perfect crime.

Armed with a delusion of superiority, the pair began asserting their perceived immunity from normal restrictions with acts of petty theft and vandalism. They even broke into a fraternity house at the university and stole penknives, a camera, and a typewriter that they later used to type their ransom note. Emboldened, they progressed to a series of more serious crimes, including arson; but no one seemed to notice. Leopold (then 19 years old) and Loeb (18) settled on the kidnapping and murder of a young boy as their perfect crime.

---

*Planning the Murder*

---

They spent seven months planning everything from the method of abduction to disposal of the body. A chisel was selected as the murder weapon, and purchased.

The plan was simple: rent a car under an assumed name, find a wealthy victim (preferably a boy since girls were more closely watched), kill him in the car with a chisel, then dump the body in a culvert. Even though the victim was to be killed immediately, Leopold and Loeb planned on a ransom from the victim's family. The victim's family would receive a letter instructing them to pay $10,000 in which they would. They spent seven months planning everything from the method of abduction to disposal of the body. A chisel was selected as the murder weapon, and purchased later be asked to throw from a moving train.

Interestingly, Leopold and Loeb spent a lot more time on figuring out how to retrieve the ransom than on who their victim was to be. After considering a number of specific people to be their victim, including their own fathers, Leopold and Loeb decided to leave the choice of victim up to chance and circumstance.

They decided upon Robert Bobby Franks, the 14-year-old son of wealthy Chicago watch manufacturer Jacob Franks. Loeb knew Bobby Franks well; he was his second cousin, an across-the-street neighbor, and had played tennis at the Loeb residence several times.

---

*The Murder*

---

On May 21, 1924, Leopold and Loeb were ready to put their plan into action. After renting a Willys-Knight automobile and covering its license plate, Leopold and Loeb needed a victim. Around 5 o'clock, Leopold and Loeb spotted 14-year-old Bobby Franks, who was walking home from school.

Loeb, who knew Bobby Franks because he was both a neighbor and a distant cousin, lured Franks into the car by asking Franks to discuss a new tennis racket (Franks loved to play tennis). Once Franks had climbed into the front seat of the car, the car took off.

Within minutes, Franks was struck several times in the head with a chisel, dragged from the front seat into the back, and then had a cloth shoved down his throat. Laying limply on the floor of the back seat, covered with a rug, Franks died from suffocation. As Franks lay dying or dead in the backseat, Leopold and Loeb drove toward a hidden culvert in the marshlands near Wolf Lake, a location known to Leopold because of his birding expeditions. On the way, Leopold and Loeb stopped twice. Once to strip Franks' body of clothing and another time to buy dinner. Once it was dark with the body on the floorboard out of view, they drove to their predetermined dumping spot near Wolf Lake in Hammond, Indiana, 25 miles south of Chicago. Leopold and Loeb found the culvert, shoved Franks' body inside the drainage pipe after they removed and discarded Franks' clothes To obscure the body's identification they poured hydrochloric acid on the face, and on a distinctive abdominal scar, as well as the genital area (to conceal the fact that he was circumcised).

---

*Ransom Note*

---

By the time the two men returned to Chicago, word had already spread that Franks was missing. Leopold called Franks' mother, identifying himself as George Johnson, and told her that Franks had been kidnapped; instructions for delivering the ransom would follow. After mailing the typed ransom note, burning their blood-stained clothing, and cleaning the bloodstains from the rented vehicle's upholstery as best they could, they spent the remainder of the evening playing cards.

Once the Franks family received the ransom note the following morning, Leopold called a second time and dictated the first set of ransom payment instructions. The ransom idea was abandoned when word came that a man named Tony Minke had found the body. Their kidnapping exposed, Leopold and Loeb destroyed the stolen typewriter and burned a robe used to move the body. Convinced that they had done everything they could to hide their tracks, they went about their lives as usual.

---

*Arrest*

---

Leopold and Loeb thought that the culvert would keep the body hidden until it had been reduced to a skeleton. However, on that dark night, Leopold and Loeb didn't realize that they had placed Franks' body with the feet sticking out of the drainage pipe. The following morning, the body was discovered and quickly identified. With the body found, the police now had a location to start searching. Near the culvert, the police found a pair of glasses, which turned out to be specific enough to be traced back to Leopold. When confronted about the glasses, Leopold explained that the glasses must have fallen out of his jacket when he fell during a birding excavation. Although Leopold's explanation was plausible, the police continued to look into Leopold's whereabouts. Leopold said he had spent the day with Loeb. It didn't take long for Leopold and Loeb's alibis to break down.

It was discovered that Leopold's car, which they had said they had driven around all day in, had been actually been at home all day. Leopold's chauffeur had been fixing it. On May 31, just ten days after the murder, both 18-year-old Loeb and 19-year-old Leopold confessed to the murder.

Loeb confessed first. He asserted that Leopold had planned everything, and had killed Franks in the back seat of the car while he, Loeb, drove. Leopold's confession followed swiftly; but he insisted that he was the driver, and Loeb the murderer. Their confessions otherwise corroborated most of the evidence in the case. Leopold later claimed that he pleaded in vain with Loeb to admit to killing Franks. While most observers believed that Loeb did indeed strike the fatal blows, some circumstantial evidence, including testimony from eyewitness Carl Ulvigh, who said he saw Loeb driving and Leopold in the back seat minutes before the kidnapping suggested that Leopold could have been the killer.

Both admitted that they were driven by the thrill of the kill and their aspiration to commit a perfect crime. Leopold, at least, considered the incident an intellectual exercise.

## *Trial*

The young age of the victim, the brutality of the crime, the wealth of the participants, and the confessions, all made this murder front page news. With the public decidedly against the boys and an extremely large amount of evidence tying the boys to the murder, it was almost certain that Leopold and Loeb were going to receive the death penalty. Fearing for his nephew's life, Loeb's uncle went to famed defense attorney Clarence Darrow and begged him to take the case. Darrow was not asked to free the boys, for they were surely guilty; instead, Darrow was asked to save the boys' lives by getting them life sentences rather than the death penalty. The judge was persuaded; in September 1924 he sentenced both men to life imprisonment for the murder, and an additional 99 years for the kidnapping. Less than a month later Loeb's father died of heart failure.

On July 21, 1924, the trial against Leopold and Loeb began. Most people thought Darrow would plead them not guilty by reason of insanity, but in a surprising last minute twist, Darrow had them plead guilty. The prosecution had over 80 witnesses that presented the cold blooded murder in all its gory details. The defense focused on psychology, especially the boys' upbringing. After listening to all the evidence presented and thinking carefully on the matter, Judge Caverly announced his decision on September 19, 1924. Judge Caverly sentenced Leopold and Loeb to jail for 99 years for kidnapping and for the rest of their natural lives for murder. He also recommended that they never be eligible for parole.

## *The Prison Life and Deaths of Leopold and Loeb*

Leopold and Loeb were originally separated, but by 1931 they were again close. In 1932, Leopold and Loeb opened a school in the prison to teach other prisoners. On January 28, 1936, Loeb was attacked in the shower by his cellmate. He was slashed over 50 times with a straight razor and died of his wounds.

Leopold became a model prisoner. He reportedly mastered 12 languages in addition to the 15 he already spoke and made multiple significant contributions to improving conditions at Stateville Penitentiary. These included reorganizing the prison library, revamping the schooling system and teaching its students, and volunteer work in the prison hospital. In 1944 Leopold volunteered for the Stateville Penitentiary Malaria Study; he was deliberately inoculated with malaria pathogens, then subjected to multiple experimental malaria treatments. He was paroled in March of 1958 and moved to Puerto Rico, where he married in 1961. Subsequently he earned a master's degree at the University of Puerto Rico, then taught classes there; became a researcher in the social service program of Puerto Rico's department of health; worked for an urban renewal and housing agency; and did research in leprosy at the University of Puerto Rico's school of medicine. Leopold died on August 30, 1971 from a heart attack.

# 9.0 Immortality

Vampire- night creature, immortal, can't have children, feast on blood.

Werewolf- transformations, slow mortal, day or n night walkers.

Perhaps, just a normal immortal.

## Pro

Always time to seek knowledge

See changes of man

Never fearing illness or death

Accomplish all dreams and goals

## con

never escape life with death

see the fall of man

everyone you know will always die

love would never last forever

## 10.0 Wisdom

Imagine having the wisdom of a lifetime while we were young. Being granted wisdom naturally at birth. Would be make the mistakes that the young do to learn and grow? Would we take opportunity and risk for better choices? Would that cure sadness and bitterness among our hearts? But what is life but an adventure and learning. How do we learn without mistakes? Would out sense of adventure be lost in careful wise steps?

What if we had all the knowledge there was to have? Would we use this all to benefit and fix our planet and mankind would we reverse the damages we have done to ourselves? Would we use it like human nature has shown and try to control what we are not meant to? Are we really supposed to have the answers to all of life's mysteries? Would that destroy hope and turn faith into science?

## 11.0 Questioning my purpose

Have you ever stopped and wondered if the path you are on is the right one? Why we are here and what our purpose of being on this earth is? What I'm meant to do and be. If your mistakes and regrets changed you for the better. If changing the past would really have any benefit to you now. Do you wonder if you have truly found yourself? Know yourself. Having inner peace and true happiness. Do you wonder where you may find yourself in the future? Will I be happy with life in my old age or bitter with regrets and missed opportunities?

Time flew by so quickly I still feel 20 at thirty. I stop and wonder if this was what I really wanted or envisioned at this point in my life. Where do I go for here? Perhaps an early midlife crisis. Trying to find my place in this world again. Trying to analyze where I am and where I want to be. Realizing I am not the same person I was at twenty. Realizing how much I've grown and changed. Contemplating a bucket list and how I should live my days. Time seems to fly. I'm curious about the impact I've made but just don't know it. Is this where I am meant to be? Is this as good as it gets?

Why haven't I found myself by now and why do I still let the past influence the now and future.

## 12.0 Bermuda Triangle

The Bermuda Triangle, also known as the Devil's Triangle, is a loosely defined region in the western part of the North Atlantic Ocean, where a number of aircraft and ships are said to have disappeared under mysterious circumstances. According to the US Navy, the triangle does not exist, and the name is not recognized by the US Board on Geographic Names. Popular culture has attributed various disappearances to the paranormal or activity by extraterrestrial beings. Documented evidence indicates that a significant percentage of the incidents were inaccurately reported or embellished by later authors a 2013 study, the World Wide Fund for Nature identified the world's 10 most dangerous waters for shipping, but the Bermuda Triangle was not among them.

*Triangle Area*

The first written boundaries date from an article by Vincent Gaddis in 1964 where the triangle's three vertices are in Miami, Florida peninsula; in San Juan, Puerto Rico; and in the mid-Atlantic island of Bermuda. But subsequent writers did not follow this definition. Some writers give different boundaries and vertices to the triangle, with the total area varying from 500,000 sq. miles to 1,500,000 sq. miles. Consequently, the determination of which accidents have occurred inside the triangle depends on which writer reports them. The United States Board on Geographic Names does not recognize this name, and it is not delimited in any map drawn by US government agencies. The area is one of the most heavily traveled shipping lanes in the world, with ships crossing through it daily for ports in the Americas, Europe, and the Caribbean Islands. Cruise ships are also plentiful, and pleasure craft regularly go back and forth between Florida and the islands. It is also a heavily flown route for commercial and private aircraft heading towards Florida, the Caribbean, and South America from points north.

The earliest allegation of unusual disappearances in the Bermuda area appeared in a September of 1950 in a published article Two years later a short article by George Sand covering the loss of several planes and ships, including the loss of Flight 19, a group of five U.S. Navy Avenger bombers on a training mission. Sand's article was the first to lay out the now-familiar triangular area where the losses took place. Flight 19 alone would be covered again in 1962 issue of a popular magazine. Sand's article was the first to suggest a supernatural element to the area. In a 1964 publication Vincent Gaddis' article The Deadly Bermuda Triangle argued that disappearances were part of a pattern of strange events in the region. Others would follow with their own works, elaborating on Gaddis' ideas all keeping to some of the same supernatural elements.

Researchers argued that many claims of writers were often exaggerated and unverifiable. Often the research was simple. Review of period newspapers of the dates of the reported incidents and on possibly relevant events like unusual weather that was never mentioned in the disappearance stories. It had theoretically been concluded that the number of ships and aircraft reported missing in the area was not significantly greater than in any other part of the ocean. In an area frequented by tropical storms, the number of disappearances that did occur were not mysterious and writers would often fail to mention such storms. Some disappearances had never happened. One plane crash was said to have taken place in 1937 off Florida, in front of witnesses, but a check of the local papers revealed nothing. They were able to show that some of the pro-paranormal material is often misleading or inaccurate. Finally, if the Triangle is assumed to cross land, such as parts of Puerto Rico, the Bahamas, or Bermuda itself, there is no evidence for the disappearance of any land-based vehicles or persons. The city of Freeport, located inside the Triangle, operates a major shipyard and an airport that handles 50,000 flights annually and is visited by over a million tourists a year, yet nothing paranormal has been recorded here.

Triangle writers have used a number of supernatural concepts to explain the events. One explanation pins the blame on leftover technology from the mythical lost continent of Atlantis. Sometimes connected to the Atlantis story is the submerged rock formation known as the Bimini Road off the island of Bimini in the Bahamas, which is in the Triangle by some definitions. Followers of the purported psychic Edgar Cayce take his prediction that evidence of Atlantis would be found in 1968 as referring to the discovery of the Bimini Road. Believers describe the formation as a road, wall, or other structure, though geologists consider it to be of natural origin. Other writers attribute the events to UFOs. This idea was used by Steven Spielberg for his film Close Encounters of the Third Kind, which features the lost Flight 19 aircrews as alien abductees. Others suggest sudden rogue tidal waves. Or maybe some mysterious geomagnetic anomaly that creates navigational problems confusing pilots and somehow causing them to plunge into the ocean; then again, pilots are trained to fly even with a loss of electronic navigation, and that theory doesn't explain ship disappearances.

---

*Natural Explanations*

---

Compass problems are one of the cited phrases in many Triangle incidents. While some have theorized that unusual local magnetic anomalies may exist in the area, such anomalies have not been found. Magnetic north and geographic north are only exactly the same for a small number of places; for example, in the United States only those places running on a line from Wisconsin to the Gulf of Mexico are these the same. But the public may not be as informed, and think there is something mysterious about a compass changing across an area as large as the Triangle, which it naturally will.

The Gulf Stream is a deep ocean current that originates in the Gulf of Mexico and then flows through the Straits of Florida into the North Atlantic. In essence, it is a river within an ocean, it has a velocity of up to 5.6 miles per hour. A small plane making a water landing or a boat having engine trouble can be carried away from its reported position by the current.

One of the most cited explanations in official inquiries as to the loss of any aircraft or vessel is human error. Human stubbornness may have caused businessman Harvey Conover to lose his sailing yacht, the Revonoc, as he sailed into the teeth of a storm south of Florida in 1958.

Tropical cyclones are powerful storms, which form in tropical waters and have historically cost thousands of lives lost and caused billions of dollars in damage. These storms have in the past caused a number of incidents related to the Triangle.

An explanation for some of the disappearances has focused on the presence of large fields of periodic methane eruptions (sometimes called mud volcanoes) on the shelves. Laboratory experiments carried out in Australia have proven that bubbles can, indeed, sink a scale model ship by decreasing the density of the water; any wreckage consequently rising to the surface would be rapidly dispersed by the Gulf Stream. Publications describe large stores of undersea hydrates worldwide.

The incident resulting in the single largest loss of life in the history of the US Navy not related to combat occurred when USS Cyclops, carrying a full load of manganese ore and with one engine out of action, went missing without a trace with a crew of 309 sometime in 1918. Although there is no strong evidence for any single theory, many independent theories exist, some blaming storms, some capsizing, and some suggesting that wartime activity was to blame for the loss. In addition, two of Cyclops's sister ships, Proteus and Nereus were also lost in the North Atlantic during the same time. Both ships were transporting heavy loads of metallic ore. In all three cases structural failure due to overloading with a much denser cargo than designed is considered the most likely cause of sinking.

Flight 19 was a training flight of five TBM Avenger torpedo bombers that disappeared in 1945, while over the Atlantic. The squadron's flight plan was scheduled to take them due east from Fort Lauderdale for 141 miles, north for 73 miles, and then back over a final 140-mile leg to complete the exercise. The flight never returned to base. The disappearance is attributed by Navy investigators to navigational error leading to the aircraft running out of fuel.

In 1948, a Douglas aircraft, disappeared while on a flight from San Juan, Puerto Rico, to Miami. No trace of the aircraft or the 32 people on board was ever found. From the documentation compiled by the Civil Aeronautics Board investigation, a key to the plane's disappearance was found: the plane's batteries were inspected and found to be low on charge, this could have led to complete electrical failure.

On August 28, 1963, a pair of  Air Force aircraft collided and crashed into the Atlantic. The Triangle of this story specifies that they did collide and crash, but there were two distinct crash sites, separated by over 160 miles of water. However, research showed otherwise in an unclassified version of the Air Force investigation report.

So, while we can explain things both natural and supernatural one thing we know for sure is the planet we live on is a mysterious one. And when tragedy strikes, mankind runs away with a story to be told. True or not.

## 13.0 Variety Blogs

Blogging experts say that you should blog and focus on one subject and get to know that subject well. Why when there is so much to learn and share? So many topics that curious minds would love to devour the knowledge of. Those who have the knowledge wish to share it.

## 14.0 Can Mythical Creatures Exist?

Is it possible there is truth behind our fables and tales? Is it possible the creatures of our imagination were once seen? The fascination heightened because we cannot own, conquer, or control. Unicorns, Loch ness, mermaids, and Bigfoot. There is so much on our own planet we have yet to even find. New civilizations and creature found by science all the time.  So who is to say they didn't exist at one time or still do? Theory and science to solve the mysteries that we aren't meant to know. Could these creatures come from sightings, dreams, or delusions?

## 15.0 Superman....er..woman

If you could choose one superpower what would it be? Mindreading may be a bit of torture on the self-esteem and the view of human nature may not be so pleasant. Mind control may be fun for a while, nut could be abused. Healing would be beneficial, but will you be messing with the balance of nature? Would you be able to hide such a power without being used for that power? Speed could be dangerous for you trip or hit something. Flying. Yes I chose flying. What a better way see the world from any view.

## 16.0 Life and death

Is there life after death? Do sprits roam the earth in search of peace or just a memory imprinted that our minds can pick up on. Do we have proof? Is proof needed? The mind replays life 3-5 minutes after death, Is this what we see when our life flashed before our eyes How do you find certainty in what to believe in? How do you dedicate full trust and fate in things you cannot see? How do you know what you believe is true or a fable to encourage moral behavior. Does religion give us guidance? Do we have proof what is true and what is a story of good behaviors. How do we know before the end if what we dedicated our heart to is the true path?

## 17.0 Life without time

Certainly, happy people do not observe the hours passing, but the time does not cease to run forward, year after year, day by day, minute by minute, and second by second. Since olden times people feel the necessity to measure time, so the history of development hours has more than one millennium. And it seems that the history of clock use will never end.

Unfortunately, there is no specific person - the inventor of watches, and if there were, the humanity would be grateful to him. It is difficult to imagine even one day of life without such a useful and practical invention of human hands. Just imagine: a simple person looks at the clock about 20 times a day and a business person - two to three times more often!

In ancient times, people determined time by the sun, or rather the shadow. Someone thought to stick a stake into the ground and measure the length of its shadow. Over time, people began to divide the space surrounding the peg in regular intervals and so appeared the first quadrant in history. Maybe we would have used this system since now, if the nature hadn't been so diverse. The sundial does not work at night, in cloudy weather, on the ships in the voyage, in the woods and other places where man needs to be. So the attempts to create a more practical time counter continued.

The next step was the invention of the sand glass. Of course, they worked in rain and snow, day and night, but new problems arose. First, with such a device it could be measured only short intervals of time, and the measurements should be made continuously, so not to lose the time account. Secondly, even a small pebble fallen into the sand, could stop the passage of time. And, thirdly, the exactness of these measurements was always doubtful, because hourglass are faster if there is colder around, and more slowly if it's warmer. Obviously, the search for the universal clock continued.

And finally, was made the first step towards the rapid development of the watch industry. In Milan in 1335 were constructed the first mechanical clock. After this, the inventors couldn't stop: they improved the design, added features, complicated the aspects and competed in originality. In the XV century in Germany in the mechanism has been built a spring, which could move the clock's hour arrow, and only in the XVII century it became possible to add the minute arrow. By this time for more than one and a half century, there were used the portable, pocket clocks. Of course, it was an expensive luxury item, which was always improving. Then it was added the second arrow in the design and for the first time the dial was covered with glass.

The age of pocket clocks was replaced by the era of wrist watches. They appeared in the early 19th century and were designed only for women. Of course, men did not seek to assign this female accessory, but the convenience won! The pilots surrendered first.

Agree that is not very convenient to use the pocket clocks steering at the wheel of the aircraft. And today two-thirds of all watches, produced in the world are man's wrist watch.

There are no limits in choosing watches. It can be declared that in the XXI century clocks are no longer just instruments for measuring time, but an accessory that complements the aspect, creates a certain image and can even tell a lot about the owner. For example, cheap watches speak not only about the financial condition, but that person is not pretentious, that he can be messy and probably negligent.

Is not worth saving for the watches; the optimal price is considered which corresponds to two month's salary of the person. Those who choose round clock are often reliable and moderately conservative people. Watches with unusual shape are chosen primarily by narcissistic people, or those who want to demonstrate their individuality. Similar characteristics can be attributed to persons who wear huge wrist watches. The clock on the leather strap demonstrates that this person is refined and elegant.

If on the person's hand there is a perfectly matched to the clothes and shoes Swiss watch, he knows what he wants from life; most likely e is pedantic and purposeful. The owner of sports watches wants to demonstrate their masculinity and strength. In general, everyone, regardless of the nature, social status and taste can find something at his wishes.

- ✓ You'd use your body's circadian clock. Imagine sleeping when you're tired and eating when you're hungry, not just because it's, say, 10pm or lunch hour.
- ✓ You would party until you wanted to, not until you'd reached your curfew
- ✓ We'd be minus one phobia, because no one would suffer from chronomentrophobia.
- ✓ In an exam you'd take your own sweet time to answer questions. It really doesn't make sense to cram everything you've learnt throughout the whole year into a few hours!
- ✓ Because there'd be no clock-in time, employees would arrive and leave at different hours, thus eliminating rush hour traffic.
- ✓ You could get up when you felt like it. Imagine rising when you want to, without worrying about

whether you'll make it in time for that 8am meeting.

- ✓ You'd never know when anyone would arrive for a dinner party. And to cook the meal you were serving, you'd have to rely on your instincts to decide when it was ready.
- ✓ You could lose yourself in cyberspace. No one could measure the amount of time you're spending on Facebook or twitter.
- ✓ Hotel lobbies would look much better. Ever noticed how all those clocks displaying time in various cities of the world clutter up spaces? I suggest they invest in art instead.
- ✓ There wouldn't be any annoying clock-watchers... so no one would expect you to arrive on the dot.

## 18.0 Killer Coaster

Euthanasia Coaster is a hypothetical euthanasia machine in the form of a roller coaster, engineered to humanely—with elegance and euphoria—take the life of a human being. Riding the coaster's track, the rider is subjected to a series of intensive motion elements that induce various unique experiences: from euphoria to thrill, and from tunnel vision to loss of consciousness and eventually death. Thanks to the marriage of the advanced cross-disciplinary research in aerospace medicine, mechanical engineering, material technologies and of course gravity, the fatal journey is made pleasing, elegant and meaningful. Celebrating the limits of the human body but also the liberation from the horizontal life, this 'kinetic sculpture' is in fact the ultimate roller coaster.

John Allen, former president of the famed Philadelphia Toboggan Company, once said that the ultimate roller coaster is built when you send out twenty-four people and they all come back dead. This could be done, you know.

Just a thought……………Inspirations

Just a thought……………What makes a good human being?

Just a thought……………Being struck by lightning….Ouch

Just a thought……………Would you be a celebrity?

## 19.0 Accidently killed

What would you do if you accidently killed another? Would you run? Would you cover it up? Would you turn yourself in? Could you live with what happened?

## 20.0 Are we alien?

What if we were placed her as an alien experiment? They watch us evolve and fall. Study the nature of their creations. What If aliens do exist and taught us how to evolve and live?

## 21.0 Possessed

Demonic possession is an interesting topic. So many stories and theories, but not yet proven. It is said that the body can be taken over by other spirits both animal and demon as well as hold more than one spirit. Possession is spoken of in most all religions, legends, and countries. Each one passed off as possible mental disorder, nervous disorder, lie, or cultural time beliefs such as witch hunting. There are religious leaders in all sects who are schooled and trained on their own religions exorcism practices. I find it interesting that to this day exorcisms are still taught but you never hear of it actually happening.

## 22.0 Depression and Anxiety

Depression hurts. It hurts emotionally and physically. It cannot be helped nor cured though creativity can flow from it. They say the most famous of writers and painters suffer from such. Counseling and medications can help, but can also make I work by thinking you are low or crazy wrought need help. Hating taking pills to deal with life. Hating the symptoms and dealing with the side effects. Always sad and no motivation. Always tired and never being as excited about things a think you should be. Jay is harder to find/ Inner peace is so far way. There is always a hole or void that you always try to fill without success. It seems like nothing you do is ever right. Every joke is criticism. Every compliment a lie. Every complaint geared towards you. Everything is bad and happens to you because you feel cursed. Your mind always races and you never stop searching for your own cure.

## 23.0 Teenager

A tornado of emotion and change while calm and normal one moment and rampaging and angry the next. Changing g so fast you are sure that you know your own child anymore. Opinions sometimes make no sense. Heartfelt one moment and judgmental the next. Argumentative and not sure why. Pulling away from hugs and kisses. Makes you proud then breaks your trust. Like talking to a wall when explaining life and growing advice.

## 24.0 Doppelgangers

In fiction and folklore, doppelganger is a paranormal double of a living person. It also describes the sensation of having glimpsed oneself with no chance of the supposed phenomenon having been a reflection. A doppelgänger is often perceived as a sinister form and is regarded by some to be of bad luck. In some traditions, a doppelganger seen by a person's relative or friend portends illness or danger while seeing one's own doppelganger is said to be an omen of death.

The current version is often used in a more general sense to identify any person that physically or behaviorally resembles another person without regard to the word's original paranormal meaning, thus shifting it back to the original German meaning of look-alikes. Although this German word is of recent origin, first appearing in English use in 1851, the concept of alter egos and double spirits appears in the folklore, myths, religious concepts, and traditions of many cultures throughout human history.

In Ancient Egyptian mythology, a doppelganger having the same memories and feelings as the person to whom the counterpart belongs. In Norse mythology, a doppelganger is a ghostly double that precedes a living person and is seen performing their actions in advance. In some myths, the doppelgänger is a personification of death. It is also suggested that the phenomenon created is seen in certain mental illnesses, such as schizophrenia, particularly when accompanied by paranoia.

It was also claimed that a dream or illusion had haunted Abraham Lincoln at times through the winter. On the evening of his election he had thrown himself on one of the sofas at his home, just after the first telegrams of November 7 had told him he was elected president, and looking into a bureau mirror across the room he saw himself full length, but with two faces. It bothered him; he got up; the illusion vanished; but when he lay down again there in the glass again were two faces, one paler than the other. He got up again, mixed in the election excitement, forgot about it; but it came back, and haunted him. He told his wife about it; she worried too. A few days later he tried it once more and the illusion of the two faces were seen again. But that was the last; the ghost since then wouldn't come back, he told his wife, who said it was a sign he would be elected to a second term, and the death pallor of one face meant he wouldn't live through his second term. Lincoln was known to be superstitious, and old mirrors will occasionally produce double images; whether this illusion can be counted as a doppelganger is perhaps debatable, though probably no more than other such claims of doppelgängers. An alternate consideration, however, suggests that Lincoln suffered vertical strabismus in his left eye, which is a disorder that could cause visions of vertical double images.

A famous Victorian apparition was the strange appearance of Vice-Admiral Sir George Tryon. He walked through the drawing room of his family home in London, looking straight ahead, without exchanging a word to anyone, in front of several guests at a party being given by his wife on 22 June 1893 whilst he was supposed to be in a ship of the Mediterranean Squadron, maneuvering off the coast of Syria. Subsequently it was reported that he had gone down with his ship, that very same night, after it had collided with another ship following an unexplained order to turn the ship in the direction of the other vessel.

## 25.0 The view of an Atheist

Edgar Allan Poe, Sigmund Freud, Einstein, Thomas Edison were all atheists. Emily Dickenson as well. All born in a time when it was wrong not to believe in something. Are all these books and religions yet just stories to improve behavior and teach morality?

"When it's obvious that goals cannot be reached, don't adjust goals, adjust action steps" Confucius

"Science predicts that many different kinds of universe will be spontaneously created out of nothing. It is a matter of chance which we have become" Stephen Hawking.

## Just a thought.........The mystery of Human Combustion

## Just a thought......Homeless.... Could you survive?

## 26.0 Fears

I fear for failure. I fear not being remembered. I fear losing those that I love as I get older. I fear what I may not be able to handle. I fear my inner demons may haunt me forever and I'll never overcome my past. I fear tragic death, but not peaceful death. I fear destitution. I fear disaster and if I could survive it.

## 27.0 Unsolved murders; how would you handle it?

What could be worse than never knowing what happened? Never having answers and searching for the rest of your days when a loved one disappears. Are they alive? Are they dead? How long must you wait before you know? Always looking in the crowd for their face. Always waiting to hear their voice. Always waiting for some sort of sign. How could you ever really go back to living normal again? Perhaps they purposely disappeared. Would you be angry if they came back? How could you not be haunted by these thoughts daily?

## 28.0 Homeless Hero

Elizabeth Murray, born September 23, 1980, is an inspirational speaker who is notable for having been accepted by Harvard University despite being homeless in her high school years. Murray was born in the Bronx, New York to poor and drug-addicted parents, both of whom would later contract HIV. Some of her earliest memories are of her parents spending their welfare payments on cocaine and heroin when she and her sister were starving. She became homeless just after she turned 15, when her mother died of AIDS and was buried in a donated wooden box. Liz's father failed to pay the rent on their flat and her father moved to a homeless shelter. Liz was out on the streets. Her sister got a place on a friend's sofa, but Liz slept on the city's 24-hour underground trains or on park benches. When she became homeless at 16, as well as stealing food she would shoplift self-help books and study for exams in a friend's hallway. Liz would turn up to school lice-ridden and was bullied for being smelly and scruffy and eventually dropped out. Despite personal adversity, Murray began attending the Humanities Preparatory Academy in Chelsea, Manhattan. Despite her late high school start and lack of a stable home she did a year's work a term and went to night classes. A teacher saw her gumption and mentored her. Murray graduated in two years. She was awarded a New York Times scholarship for needy students and was accepted into Harvard University, matriculating in the fall semester of 2000. Her older sister Lisa graduated from Purchase College in New York State and is a school teacher for children with autism.

In late 2006, her father died of AIDS. She returned to Harvard in 2006 and graduated in June 2009. As of August 2009, she began taking graduate courses at Harvard Summer School with plans to earn a doctorate in clinical psychology and become a counselor.

She is the founder and director of Manifest Living. A made-for-TV film about Murray's life Homeless to Harvard: The Liz Murray Story, was released in 2003. On May 19, 2013, she was awarded an honorary doctorate of public service and gave the commencement address at Merrimack College in North Andover, Massachusetts. A woman who overcame tremendous odds to go from "homeless to Harvard" has turned her life story into an American bestseller.

## 29.0 Places you will never visit

Cheap air travel has allowed us the opportunity to reach almost any spot on the planet within a matter of hours. But no matter how widely you travel, there are some places you are never going to get to visit.

---

*Snake Island*

*Sao Paulo State, Brazil*

---

Perhaps unsurprisingly, this small island has become known as Snake Island and only doughty scientists and crazed adventurers dare set foot on its ground.

Snake Island is home to a vast colony of golden lance head pit vipers among the most poisonous snakes on the planet. The golden lance head is only to be found on this one particular island, so it is understandably rather protective of its territory. Its venom is about five times as potent as that of its cousin, which is itself responsible for more South American snakebite deaths than any other species.

Just getting to the island, which covers about 45 hectares, takes considerable determination. It is first necessary to cross a 30-kilometres stretch of choppy water from the coast of the Brazilian state of São Paulo, and there are few local sea captains willing to make the trip. Once at the island, there is no beach to speak of, and access is via a steep, rocky slope covered in hand-mincing barnacles. All of which is somewhat academic, given that the Brazilian Navy expressly forbids civilians from landing there anyway. Only accredited scientists are occasionally given special dispensation to visit.

There are at least 5000 snakes writhing around the place, with conservative estimates suggesting one for every square meter: they have even taken over a now-defunct lighthouse. Being lighthouse keeper here surely ranked high among the worst jobs in the world. Legend has it that the last keeper lived there with his family until snakes got into their cottage. As they tried to flee, they were taken out one by one by vipers dangling from the branches of overhanging trees. Myth or not, the best advice is to leave their home as it is.

---

*Menwith Hill*

*North Yorkshire, England*

---

Menwith Hill is a base belonging to the UK Ministry of Defense, but made available to the US Department of Defense, who are responsible for many elements of its running. As part of America's global defense communications network, Menwith's stated mission is to provide intelligence support for the United States, UK and their allied interests. However, some question the extent of its powers. Built on land owned by the British War Office, Menwith Hill became operational in 1960. From the beginning, however, Menwith Hill was staffed by US military personnel under the remit of the US Army Security Agency. Menwith Hill has always been at the technological cutting edge, and in its early days was used to monitor communications coming out of the Soviet bloc. It was also an early adopter of IBM computer technology. Today, the site is home to large numbers of multi-faceted radar crucial to the ability of the US and UK to intercept and monitor communications. Menwith Hill is widely believed to form part of the fabled ECHELON global surveillance network. ECHELON is said to be able to 'eavesdrop' on all types of modern communication, from telephone conversations to email exchanges. It is alleged that the network operates under the agreement of the governments of Britain, the US, Australia, Canada and New Zealand. A 2001 report by the European Parliament into the alleged network concluded that Menwith Hill was its single biggest facility. While the gathering of such information to thwart terrorism or organized crime may seem attractive, many fear that other information gleaned can be too easily abused. Some have suggested it could be used for industrial espionage, while others are concerned about the implications for civil liberties. Several journalists have cited instances of American companies gaining commercial advantage over European counterparts, though none of these cases were ever conclusively proved. In 2007, the base drew further unwanted attention after the British government confirmed that it would be upgraded to provide early warning of missile attacks as part of a planned US missile defense system. A perimeter fence is dotted with watchtowers and patrolled by guards and trained dogs. In the popular imagination, this facility is filled with spies scanning our private conversations and intruding on the intimate details of our daily lives. Whether deserved or not, Menwith Hill has a reputation as the ultimate Big Brother, listening in on what everybody else is saying, but with not a lot to say for itself.

---

*The Queen's bedroom, Buckingham Palace*

*Westminster, London, England*

---

Buckingham Palace is the British Queen's official London residence, and one of the most iconic buildings in the world. Yet despite attracting hordes of tourists, large swathes of the labyrinthine palace remain under the highest security and off-limits to the world at large. Most private of all is the Queen's personal bedroom, once the scene of a notorious break-in. Buckingham Palace was originally plain old Buckingham House, built as the London pad of the Duke of Buckingham in 1705. The location he chose had once been a mulberry garden where King James I had attempted to rear silkworms. The house took the fancy of King George III, who purchased it as a residence for his wife, Queen Charlotte. It only became a palace in the 1820s, after monarch George IV ordered extensive renovations from an architect. George, though, would never live in it, and so Queen Victoria became the first monarch to take up residence when she moved in during July 1837. After the young queen married Prince Albert in 1840 and started a family, it was soon clear that the palace needed to be extended. Their greatest contribution was the addition of the East Wing, complete with the famous balcony from which the royals wave to their subjects at times of celebration. One such occasion marked the end of the Second World War, during which the Palace had received nine direct hits from German bombers.

Today, the Palace encompasses some 775 rooms, of which 52 are royal and guest bedrooms. When in residence, the Queen and Prince occupy a suite of rooms in the Palace's North Wing. By rights, this should be the single most impenetrable part of the building. But being such a famous landmark, Buckingham Palace has tempted many to test its security over the years, from naked paragliders to undercover journalists, and from paternal rights campaigners dressed as Batman to Osama bin Laden look-alikes. One man found on the grounds in 1990 even ambitiously claimed to be Prince Andrew and that he was there to visit his 'Mum'. But the most serious breach came on 9 July 1982, when the Queen found herself engaged in conversation in her bedroom for a good ten minutes with an intruder named Michael Fagan. In fact, this was not Fagan's first visit to the Palace, since he had successfully scaled the barbed-wire-topped perimeter wall several weeks earlier. On that occasion, on June 7th, he had wandered around the palace unhindered, even stopping to enjoy some wine, cheese and biscuits. When he returned in July, he shinned up a drain pipe into the Queen's private apartments. It was reported that his activities did trigger an alarm, but a palace employee assumed the alarm system was faulty. The armed police officer who should have been on guard outside her room was apparently out walking the dogs, and his replacement had not yet got to his position.

The first the Queen knew of a strange man in her bedroom was when she noticed the curtains twitch. Showing admirable calm, she proceeded to chat amicably with him as he walked across her chamber and perched on the end of her bed. After a while, he requested a cigarette but, perhaps unsurprisingly, the Queen did not have a packet to hand, so she requested some be brought in. This provided her with the opportunity to raise the alarm and a footman dutifully appeared on the scene, holding Fagan until the police arrived to arrest him. Fagan was subsequently charged with civil offences and spent several months in a high-security mental health facility. It was the first time that an intruder had made it into the private royal apartments since the reign of Queen Victoria (though during the Second World War the Queen Mother had stumbled upon an army deserter in her bathroom). The incident brought the issue of the Queen's security under blazing scrutiny, and the level of protection surrounding her became even greater. As well as armed guards throughout the Palace, presumably now issued with clear instructions on when they can take the corgis out. There are regular police dog patrols and a permanent detachment from the Queen's Guard, instantly recognizable in their red tunics and bearskins. In 2004, Scotland Yard took over responsibility for security at royal sites from the security services. The same year, an electric fence was erected around the Palace, administering a shock strong enough to disable an intruder until they are apprehended.

---

*Chapel of the Ark of the Covenant*

*Northern Ethiopia*

---

Access restricted: the purported home of the Ark of the Covenant. The Ark of the Covenant is described in the biblical Book of Exodus as the chest that contained the tablets of stone inscribed with the Ten

Commandments which Moses brought down from Mount Sinai. The Ark disappeared from Jerusalem long ago under mysterious circumstances and believers claim it came to Axum in Ethiopia during the reign of Menelik I in the mid-tenth century B.Th. Ark is of immense symbolic value, documented not only in the Bible but featuring also in Judaic and Islamic scripture. While its fate has long been argued over, Ethiopia's authorities say it has resided at Axum for centuries, and now lies in a specially built treasury next to the Church of St Mary of Zion. The treasury is kept under heavy guard and surrounded by fencing, all under the watchful eye of a High Priest who is the only man permitted to enter the chapel.

This virtuous elderly monk is given the post for life, and is expected to name a successor on his deathbed. The Ark used to be released for a public procession once a year. The Book of Exodus tells how the Ark was built in accordance with instructions from God. Measuring a little over 1 meter long and 70 centimeters wide and high, it was constructed from acacia wood and covered with gold. Two long rods of acacia and gold were used to carry it, and two sculptures of winged cherubim surmounted on the lid were said to keep guard over it. According to the Bible, the Ark was carried (covered in skins and cloths so that no one could set eyes on it) out of Egypt during the exodus of the Israelites. The Book of Joshua also describes its key role in the fall of Jericho. It was later said to have been captured by the Philistines (who returned it to the Israelites after being smitten with a series of plagues), while Solomon worshipped in front of it after he had his dream in which God promised him wisdom. The royal chronicles of Ethiopia, which were written in the 13th century and undoubtedly served as propaganda for the reigning dynasty of that time, hold that the Ark came to Ethiopia with Menelik, said to be the son of King Solomon and the Queen of Sheba. The story tells that a forgery of the Ark was left back in Solomon's Temple in Jerusalem, where it was presumed destroyed after the Babylonian sack of Jerusalem in 586 BC.

Meanwhile, the city of Axum became the focal point of the Kingdom of Axum, which was a leading regional power from the mid-second century BC to the tenth century AD. To this day, huge granite obelisks, the tallest single pieces of stone quarried and raised in the ancient world, tell of just how important the area was. If the Ark really was in Ethiopia at this point, Axum would have certainly made a suitable home. The Axumite king Ezana converted to Christianity in AD 331, and had the first Church of St Mary built some 40 years later. According to tradition, the Ark remained at Axum until the 16th century, when it was hidden after the city came under Muslim attack. It was returned in the following century, and in 1965 Ethiopian leader Haile Selassie had the current treasury built to house it.

There are plenty of people who do not believe that the treasure at Axum is the real Ark at all. Alternative theories about its location abound. These include a cave in Mount Nebo in Jordan, Chartres Cathedral or the village of Rennes-le-Château in France, Temple Herdewyke in England, the Basilica of St John Lateran in Rome and the Dumghe Mountains of South Africa. The Indiana Jones movie Raiders of the Lost Ark, meanwhile, proposes that the Ark found its way to Egypt.We will probably never know for certain whether Axum is home to the true Ark of the

Covenant. What is more certain is that the contents of the treasury are considered sacred by vast numbers of people, and no one has yet provided conclusive proof that it is not the true Ark.

---

### *Dulce Base*

*Rio Arriba County, New Mexico, USA*

---

Existence unacknowledged but believed by some to be home of an underground extraterrestrial base. Few places have captured the imagination of conspiracy theorists more than Dulce Base. A site for which there is little concrete evidence, believers nonetheless place it at the heart of a conspiracy between the powers-that-be and alien life forms intent on carrying out despicable research on human subjects. Whether it exists or not, Dulce Base is an instructive case study of the way conspiracy theories can take hold. Rumors of a secret base beneath a New Mexico mountain can be traced back most clearly to Paul Bennewitz, a technological entrepreneur with a side line as an investigator of unidentified flying objects. Beginning in the 1970s, Bennewitz claimed that he regularly saw strange light displays in the sky, which he believed might be linked to the Kirtland Air Force Base a little outside his native Albuquerque.

Bennewitz was not alone in claiming to have seen strange night-time light shows. Around this time, New Mexico threw up a number of other apparently unexplained phenomena, including multiple instances of cattle maiming. Bennewitz is said to have made contact with a woman who, under hypnosis, described how she and her son were kidnapped by extraterrestrials and taken to an underground lab where she witnessed cattle being mutilated. The woman also claimed to have been fitted with an implant that left her subject to mind control. Bennewitz was taken with her story and continued to compile evidence, including apparent video footage of lights in the night sky. He also constructed a system of radio receivers, and produced tapes that he said were UFO transmissions. Sometime towards the end of 1980, he contacted the authorities at Kirtland to make them aware of what he regarded as a potential UFO threat.

His claims were met with a degree of skepticism, and received only limited follow-up.

However, Bennewitz was not to be dissuaded from his suspicions. Indeed, they developed until in 1982 they drew the attention of the Aerial Phenomena Research Organization (APRO), a long-established and scientifically credible UFO-study group. William Moore, one of APRO's most senior figures, established a friendship with Bennewitz, who by now had concluded that two types of aliens had made it to Earth: good ones known as 'whites' and evil ones known as 'grays'. The grays were inhabiting a deep underground base, he told Moore, beneath Archuleta Mesa, near Dulce. Dulce is a small town in the Jicarilla Apache Reservation, close to the New Mexico-Colorado border. With a population hovering around 2,500, it is, all in all, a quiet, out-of-the-way and unassuming sort of place. Nearby stands the impressive mountain of Archuleta Mesa, with a peak of 2800 meters. According to Bennewitz, the grays had reached agreement with the White House to carry out experiments on Earth-based life forms in a specially constructed base beneath the mountain.

Over the course of the 1980s, Moore provided Bennewitz with 'evidence' to back up his suspicions, and helped him publicize his story that aliens had arrived on Earth and, with the complicity of the US government, were experimenting on humans and perfecting forms of mind control. Needless to say, Bennewitz was treated by many as simply a crank. Then, in 1989, Moore publicly declared that he had been part of a scheme to supply Bennewitz with disinformation. The only motive for this plot seems to have been to assist Bennewitz in utterly discrediting himself. Bennewitz, meanwhile, suffered deteriorating mental health until his death in 2003.So Dulce Base, for which no one has ever produced hard physical evidence, seems like nothing so much as a figment of Bennewitz's imagination. But for many, a fundamental question remains, if false, why go to all that effort of undermining him? Had he, some wonder, stumbled upon something that may have been wholly unrelated to extraterrestrials, but which the authorities didn't want him sniffing around? Was the misinformation really a case of misdirection, and the Dulce Base rumor a cover for something equally startling?

*Wildenstein Art Collection*

*Headquartered in Paris.*

It is said to be the most valuable private art collection in the world. Many art collectors are more than willing to show off their prized pieces, but that is not something that could be said of the Wildenstein family. These French multi-millionaires jealously guard the precise details of a collection that has been built up over more than a century, despite their position as perhaps the most famous family in the art world. The Wildenstein art dynasty began with Nathan Wildenstein in the 1870s. A French cloth merchant by trade, he educated himself in 18th-century painting, and took advantage of a sleeping market to earn a fortune. From his base in Paris, he had extended his empire of galleries to New York, London and Buenos Aires by the end of the 1920s. After Nathan's death, his son Georges moved the family's center of operations to the USA in 1940.The family has been long established as one of the leading suppliers to major galleries and museums throughout the world, but details of the

Wildenstein's total holdings (and their locations) are scant. It has been speculated that the collection is split between secure locations in New York, Paris, London, Buenos Aires and Tokyo, and may include some 10,000 works. Divorce proceedings in 1999 between Alec Wildenstein and his wife Jocelyn (infamous for her attempts to give herself a feline appearance through plastic surgery) estimated the collection's value at $US10 billion. It is thought to include works by Giotto di Bondone, Vermeer, Caravaggio, Rembrandt, Monet and Van Gogh. Further sketchy details about the collection have emerged in recent years during further legal battles between family members, and in 2011 a police raid at the Wildenstein Institute in Paris reportedly uncovered many works previously listed as stolen or missing.

*The Amber Room*

*In an underground cavern on the German-Czech border*

Site of historic mystery: an ornate room seized by the Nazis and later lost.

Sometimes described as the 'eighth wonder of the world', the Amber Room was constructed using 6 tons of amber backed with gold leaf. Once given by Prussia to Russia as a symbol of peace, it was stolen from the USSR by Nazi forces during the Second World War. In the chaos that accompanied Germany's defeat in 1945, the location of the room was lost, sparking an enduring quest to recover it.

Queen Sophia Charlotte of Hanover persuaded her husband, Friedrich I of Prussia, to commission the Amber Room for Charlottenburg Palace in Berlin. Designed in the baroque style by Andreas Schlüter, it was crafted under the supervision of a Dane, Gottfried Wolfram, between 1701 and 1709.

By the time it was finished, Sophia Charlotte had been dead for four years, and Friedrich would die, too, in 1713. He was succeeded by his son, Friedrich Wilhelm I. Keen to consolidate good relations with Peter the Great of Russia, Friedrich Wilhelm made him a gift of the room in 1716. It was packed into 18 large crates and sent to St Petersburg, where it was installed in the Winter Palace. In 1755 the Tsarina Elizabeth had it moved once more, this time to the Catherine Palace in Tsarkoye Selo.An Italian designer called Bartolemeo Francesco Rastrelli oversaw a redesign for this new space, importing yet more amber from Berlin for the job. After subsequent renovations, the room covered 55 square meters and is estimated to have been worth something approaching $US150 million in today's money.

The room remained at Tsarkoye Selo until 1941, when Hitler launched Operation Barbarossa, sending 3 million German troops into what was now the Soviet Union. Among the many crimes committed at this time, looting of art treasures was widespread. Officials at the

Catherine Palace hurriedly set about dismantling the Amber Room to put into safe storage, but as they began their work, they found the antique amber crumbled. They decided instead to cover the room in conventional wallpaper, in the hope that the Germans would fail to realize what lay behind it, but the plan was an utter failure. Within 36 hours of the arrival of German troops at the Palace, they had taken the room apart and stored it in 27 boxes that were soon transferred to Königsberg (now Kaliningrad) on the Baltic coast. Here, it was put back together again in the city's castle museum. When the tide of the war turned against Germany after 1943, the museum director was charged with once again disassembling the room and moving it to a safe place. However, in 1944 Königsberg was bombed by British forces and much of the city, including its museum, burned. The fate of the Amber Room is unknown.

Over the subsequent years, theories have abounded. Some believe that it perished in the fires or was destroyed by a direct hit. Others say it was burnt by Russian soldiers who captured the city in 1945, while another theory suggests that the room was dismantled and put to sea on a German ship that was then torpedoed and sunk. It has even been suggested that after his suicide Hitler's body was not burned in Berlin, but was buried in this legendary room. But for many, the paths lead to the town of Deutschneudorf, near the border of Saxony and the Czech Republic. In 1997, a single panel from the original room was found during a raid by German police. It belonged to the family of a soldier who was allegedly present when the room was dismantled during the war. In 2008, a team of excavators claimed that they had found a man-made chamber 20 meters below ground near Deutschneudorf and that, after conducting electromagnetic tests on the site, they were convinced it contained some 2 tons of Nazi gold. The mayor of Deutschneudorf, Heinz-Peter Haustein, said that the area is home to a vast network of underground storage rooms from the period, and that he was '90 per cent sure' that the Amber Room lies somewhere within the complex. Indeed, the area is honeycombed by old silver, tin and copper mines, so there is no shortage of hiding places. But to date, the Amber Room's location remains a mystery.

In the meantime, a reconstruction of the room may now be seen at Tsarskoye Selo in the Catherine Palace. It opened in 2003, having taken 24 years to complete. Much of the US$11 million funding for the project was donated by German companies – perhaps one day it will be possible to compare it with the original.

---

*North Sentinel Island*

*Andaman Islands, Bay of Bengal*

---

Access restricted to a remote island whose people reject contact with the outside world. North Sentinel Island, which covers only 72 square kilometers, has an indigenous population of somewhere between 50 and 400 Sentinelese, a dark-skinned and short-statured people and one of the last groups on earth to have resisted contact with the modern world. Jealously protective of their isolation, any attempt by outsiders to land on the island is likely to result in a hail of arrows. North Sentinel lies to the west of the southern tip of South Andaman Island and is one of 572 islands in an 800-kilometre arc. Here, the Sentinelese live as hunter-gatherers and do not seem to have developed any forms of agriculture. Their diet includes fruits, nuts, tubers, fish, wild pigs, honey and the eggs of seagulls and turtles. Their language is significantly different to any of the other tongues spoken in the island group, leading academics to conclude that they have avoided contact even with relatively near neighbors for several millennia. The island lacks any natural harbors and is surrounded by uncharted coral reefs that have largely kept out visitors as well as keeping in the Sentinelese, whose own rudimentary boats are suited only to calm lagoons.

In 1880, Maurice Portman, an administrator in the British Raj, led the first known expedition to North Sentinel. After a few days of exploration, Portman and his team captured six natives (two adults and four children), whom they took back to Port Blair, the administrative capital of the Andamans. However, the enterprise ended in disaster when the adults died from illness. The orphaned children were dispatched home loaded with presents – scant compensation for their loss. Tentative attempts from the 1960s to make contact with the Sentinelese met with limited success. Incidents such as the one in 1974 when a visiting documentary crew was attacked and the director suffered an arrow to the thigh were not uncommon. After many years of regular landings and gift offerings, the first recorded friendly contact was made in 1991.However, similar schemes with other native peoples of the islands (including the Great Andamanese and the Jarawa) had ended disastrously when those populations were decimated by exposure to common but unfamiliar diseases. Under pressure from groups arguing that the Sentinelese should not be forced into contact, the government gave up on its contact program in 1996.

---

*The Tomb of Genghis Khan*

*Assumed to be in eastern Mongolia*

---

The last resting place of the legendary Mongol leader. Given the name Temujin at birth, Genghis Khan went on to unite disparate nomadic tribes to establish the Mongol Empire, winning himself a reputation as one of history's most feared warriors in the process. In accordance with his wishes, he was buried in the utmost secrecy: the location of his tomb remains one of history's enduring conundrums, despite numerous attempts to find it. Temujin was in his mid-40s by the time he became leader of the Mongols in the early 13th century. During his reign, he laid the foundations for a vast empire that would eventually stretch from China to Hungary, taking a title, Genghis Khan, which struck fear into the hearts of both subjects and rivals. But he was more than a bloodthirsty tyrant, introducing a written language system and doing much to bring the cultures of East and West together. He died in 1227, aged around 65. The exact cause of his death is disputed, with explanations ranging from a riding accident to illness to sexual misadventure. Regardless, it was his wish to be buried in secret in accordance with tribal custom, his resting place to remain unmarked. To this end, extraordinary and infamous precautions were undertaken. Legend has it that members of his funeral escort slaughtered any person unfortunate enough to stray across their path. The slaves who built the tomb were murdered once it was completed so that they could not divulge its location, and the soldiers who killed them were in turn dispatched. It is said that the ground was then trampled by horses, planted with trees and even had a river diverted over it to hide the tomb entrance.

Debate rages as to the location of the emperor's body. Many believe that it is probably in Mongolia's Khentii Province, perhaps close to the sacred Burkhan Kaldun Mountain where Temujin was born. In 2004, an archaeological team claimed to have found his long-lost palace in this region, which many experts assume would have been close to his final resting place. In another recent project, Dr Albert Yu-Min Lin of the University of California at San Diego has attempted to harness the power of an army of internet enthusiasts, to analyze satellite images of Khentii. Yet the grave remains elusive and that is no doubt what Genghis Khan would want. According to Mongolian tradition, as long as his tomb is left undisturbed his soul will be kept protected.

---

*Woomera Prohibited Area*

---

Operations classified as it is the world's largest land-based weapons testing area.

Established in 1947, the Woomera Prohibited Area (WPA) is most famous as a huge missile testing range, but has enjoyed several different lives, including as a rocket-launch site, a spy hub and a detention center. Covering an area larger than England, its desert location has helped keep unwanted visitors away from numerous highly classified projects.

Situated several hundred kilometers northwest of Adelaide, the Woomera Prohibited Area is home to the Royal Australian Air Force (RAAF) Woomera Test Range, and is strictly off-limits to the public. It covers 127,000 square kilometers, down from a historic high of 270,000 square kilometers in 1972.The WPA began as a joint initiative between the Australian and British governments. In the aftermath of the Second World War, the UK was keen to develop a cutting-edge rocket-testing program, but lacked the space to do so. A collaboration with the Australian government that provided an opportunity to share knowledge and expenses suited all sides. Woomera was chosen as it offered a huge swathe of land largely devoid of human habitation. A mixture of desert and scrubland, temperatures regularly exceed 35°C and can go far higher. As such, the area was never conducive to mass human colonization. However, it was ideal for weapons-testing, boasting as it does mostly cloud-free skies all year round and little electromagnetic interference. The name Woomera itself derives from an Aboriginal word for a spear-throwing device.

The Joint Project, as it was known, began missile testing in earnest in 1949. This phase included nine major atomic-bomb trials that led to the nuclear contamination of an area in excess of 1,150 sq. miles. Section 400, as this area has been designated, remains strictly off-bounds on safety grounds. Environmentalists have claimed that clean-up attempts were flawed, and many Aboriginal people who were present in the region at the time of the tests allege that they are still suffering harmful effects. A town, also called Woomera, was established to support life at the WPA in 1947 – at the peak of the Joint Project, it had a population of over 7000. For much of its life, Woomera has been a closed town, accessible only to authorized inhabitants. Since 1982, it has been open to the public, but remains under the control of the Australian Department of Defense. None of Woomera's properties are privately owned: they are leased from the government and anyone considered undesirable can be asked to move on.

The Joint Project came to a halt in 1980. By then the WPA was also being used for rocket testing, playing an important role in assorted classified space programs during the 1950s and 1960s. In 1969, Australia had entered into a separate agreement with the US to construct the Nurrungar Joint Tracking Facility within the WPA. Nurrungar's three golf ball-like radomes contained huge antennae dishes and were maintained under intense security, behind razor-wire fences and complete with bullet-proof security rooms. The reason for this heightened level of protection was that Nurrungar lay at the center of a space-based surveillance program, and was key to providing early warning of Intercontinental Ballistic Missile attacks on the US. As such, it was considered a high-priority target for the Soviet Union, a fact that did not play well with an Australian public unwilling to invite the Cold War into its backyard. Some protesters claimed that Nurrungar was also used to pinpoint targets during the 1973 US bombing of Cambodia. By the time Nurrungar closed in 1999, the futures of the WPA and the town of Woomera were uncertain. The resident population was down to a few hundred, where once it had been several thousand. For a while, it looked like the construction of a migrant detention center would come to its rescue, but that too proved something of a poisoned chalice. In a four-year lifespan, the center attracted many column-inches of negative publicity for holding up to 1500 illegal immigrants in a prison camp-style setting. Inmates rioted on several occasions and some even sewed their lips together in protest at the conditions.

But in recent years, the WPA has rebounded and has never been busier in its role as the largest on-land missile testing site in the world. Buoyed by hundreds of millions of dollars of state investment since the turn of the century, its client list now includes governments and space agencies from around the world, providing bookings well into the 2020s. Although the Test Range remains at the core of the WPA, other parts of the territory are being opened up to potentially lucrative mining as there are thought to be significant quantities of gold, iron ore, opals and uranium. Anyone finding themselves in the WPA ought to keep their eyes open though. As Roger Henwood, manager of the Woomera Range, noted in 2006: 'You find a whole lot of things sticking out of the ground that supposedly never got launched.'

---

*Deborah's Gate*

*Vancouver, British Columbia*

---

Deborah's Gate is a human trafficking victims safe house run by The Salvation Army in Vancouver, British Columbia, Canada that opened in 2009. It was one of the first safe houses to open in Canada for trafficking victims who have been sexually exploited. While the primary purpose of Deborah's Gate is to aid female victims of sexual trafficking, women who have been trafficked as domestic workers may also take refuge in the safe house if there are beds available.

The safe house is named after Deborah, a biblical figure who emphasized justice and liberty. Deborah's Gate houses women, has a ten-bed capacity, and offers drug rehabilitation and refugee services The location of the safe house is kept secret in order to protect the women who stay there Both Canadian women and women from other countries are serviced by the safe house. Betty's Liberty Closet, an online store that sells women's clothing, donates 5% of all purchases to Deborah's Gate.

## 30.0 COMA

Elaine Esposa went into a coma at age 6 from an appendix operation and died in that coma 37 years later. Terry walls woke up after being in a coma after 17 years caused by a car crash. He didn’t recognize his own mother. There are 25000 to 35000 vegetative patients. They must be in a coma for more than one year to be determined vegetative. There is a phenomenon called locked in syndrome where the patient is conscious but cannot move. They can hear and see everything going on but cannot respond. Even of their brain activity shows very little activity. Research is being done to prevent patients from being unplugged when they could actually be conscious.

Nancy Crazan was in a car wreck in 1983 and thrown from the car into a ditch. She was comatose for several years and finally awoke. When she regained the ability to do so she told her family everything she had heard and said. She admitted to the fear they would let her pass even though she was still inside.

So the question remains.....if in a comatose state should the debate of continuing assisted life go on? What if we are really pulling the plug on someone simply trapped in their own body?

## 31.0 Disaster

If a major disaster occurred and everything collapsed could I survive? Would I have the strength to do what needs done for basic survival? Would I freeze or starve? Would I get mugged by other survivors because I'm too soft hearted in helping others>? Would I try to help knowing this? Where I know where to go or what to do? Would I panic?

# 32.0 Evil Experiments

Sometimes science has to be ruthless. If curing cancer means dropping a dozen frightened children into the jungle for some reason, then by God that's what you do. And if you aren't curing cancer, but are just curious about what children look like when abandoned in a jungle, well, you still do it. Why? Because science

---

*Put Kids in the Wilderness, Make Them Go to War*

---

In the summer of 1954, social psychologist Muzafer Sherif wanted to see if two groups stuck in the wild would learn to hate each other. Thus kicked off his Robbers Cave experiment, in which a group of 11 ordinary, middle-class 11-year-old boys headed to summer camp at Robbers Cave State Park in Oklahoma, anxious for three fun-filled weeks of hiking, fishing and swimming. They were completely unaware that their parents had signed them up for Sherif's experiment, and that there was a second group of campers elsewhere on the site that they would be trained to hate. To see how much conflict they could instigate between the two groups, the experimenters arranged a tournament with events like baseball and tug-of-war, promising shiny trophies and pocket knives to the winners, because as we all know, the one prize you should always award a warring band of feral children is a knife. With a little creative prodding, what started with boos and insults quickly escalated into a full-out battle, ending with the Eagles burning the Rattlers' flag after being defeated at tug-of-war.

Sherif and his team had successfully transformed 22 ordinary 11-year-old boys with no previous behavioral problems into a mob of aggressive savages. Robbers Cave was actually the third time Sherif had run the same experiment, and some sort of violence had inevitably exploded by the end of each trial? And that in one instance, the boys turned on Sherif and his team?

*Programming Kids for Violence, Then Turning Them Loose on a Clown*

In the early '60s, a psychologist named Albert Bandura wanted to investigate whether children would imitate aggressive behavior without encouragement or active suggestion. So he took a Bobo Doll or as we know them inflatable bop bags and filmed a video of an adult punching, kicking and beating the doll with hammers, because if you're going to hit a clown with something, there's no point in fucking around. Then he showed the video to a group of 24 young children. A second group was given a nonviolent video, and a third control group was given no video at all. All three groups were unleashed one at a time into a room with a Bobo Doll, some hammers and even some toy guns, though no guns were featured in either video. As seen in this clip, the kids who were shown the aggressive video wasted no time in showing Bobo exactly what they thought of his inflatable whimsy. Skeptics maintain that the children displayed a perfectly natural reaction.

One kid in the beginning even seems to be creepily whispering things to the doll at gunpoint.

The children in two other groups didn't demonstrate anywhere near as much aggression. However, Bandura's critics argued that you couldn't put children in a room with a toy that's essentially a punching bag and then claim to be proving anything. So, Bandura gathered up more children from the infinite supply of them that these scientists seem to have access to and showed them a video of an adult punching, kicking and hammering a real live clown. After watching the video, Bandura turned the kids loose into a room with a real clown. Sure enough, the children happily assaulted the man with punches, kicks and hammer blows, proving not only that kids imitate aggression, but that they have the same grasp of consequences as a death row inmate.

---

*Guilt Test*

---

Psychologists at the University of Iowa wanted to gain a better understanding of how preschoolers and toddlers experience guilt, so they devised the broken toy experiment.

The experiment was simple. An adult would show a toy to a young child. The adult would go on to explain that the toy was something very special, a sentimental item they'd had since they were very little. Then, asking the child to be very careful with it, the adult would hand over the toy. The toy was rigged to break as soon as the kid messed with it. The next part of the experiment was presumably designed to teach the children the concept of time dilation. How their guilt made it the longest damn minute they had so far experienced in their short lives. Interrogated as to why they broke the toy and how long they could stand repeating themselves.

---

*Electroshocks*

---

From early 1940 to 1953, Dr. Lauretta Bender, a highly respected child neuropsychiatrist practicing at Bellevue Hospital in New York City, experimented extensively with electroshock therapy on children who had been diagnosed with autistic schizophrenia. It has been reported that Bender administered electroconvulsive therapy to at least 100 children ranging in age from three years old to 12 years, with some reports indicating the total may be twice that number.

Bobby is seven years old, but this is not the first time he has been subjected to electroshock. It's his third time. In all, over the next year, Bobby will experience eight electroshock sessions. Placed on the examining table, he is held down by two male attendants while the physician places a solution on his temples. He begins to cry and he stiffens his body against what he knows is coming.

Despite publicly claiming good results with electroshock treatment, privately Bender said she was seriously disappointed in the after effects and results shown by the subject children. Indeed, the condition of some of the children appeared to have only worsened. One six-year-old boy, after being shocked several times, went from being a shy, withdrawn child to acting increasingly aggressive and violent. Another child, a seven-year-old girl, following five electroshock sessions had become nearly catatonic.

Years later, another of Bender's young patients who became overly aggressive after about 20 treatments, was convicted in court as a serial murderer after he had grown. Others reportedly were in and of trouble and prison for a battery of petty and violent crimes.

---

*Drug Inducing*

---

About the same time Dr. Bender was conducting her electroshock experiments, she was also widely experimenting on autistic and schizophrenic children with a wide array of psycho-pharmaceutical agents, several provided to her by the Sandoz Chemical Co. in Basel, Switzerland, as well as Metrazol, sub-shock insulin therapy, amphetamines and anticonvulsants. Metrazol was a trade name for a drug used as a circulatory and respiratory stimulant. High doses cause convulsions.

Metrazol had been used in convulsive therapy, but was never considered to be effective, and side effects such as seizures were difficult to avoid. The medical records of several patients who were confined at Vermont State Hospital, a public mental facility, reveal that Metrazol was administered to them by a contractor on numerous occasions. One of these patients, Karen Wetmore, received the drug on a number of occasions for no medical reason. During the same ten-year period in which Metrazol was used by the Vermont State Hospital, patient deaths skyrocketed. In 1982, the FDA revoked its approval of Metrazol.

It should be noted that, during the cold war years, CIA Intelligence interrogators sometimes injected large amounts of Metrazol into selected enemy or Communist agents for the purposes of severely frightening other suspected agents, by forcing them to observe the procedure. The almost immediate effects of Metrazol are shocking for many to witness as subjects would shake violently. They typically arch, jerk and contort their bodies and grimace in pain. With Metrazol, as with electroshock, bone fractures - including broken necks and backs - and joint dislocations are not uncommon, unless strong sedatives are administered beforehand.

Mary is only five years old. She sits on a small, straight-backed chair, moving her legs back and forth, humming the same four notes over and over .For the first three years of her life, Mary was thought to be a mostly normal child. Then, after she began behaving oddly, she had been handed off to a foster family. Her father and mother didn't want her any longer. She had become too strange for her father, whose alcoholism clouded any awareness of his young daughter. Mary's mother had never wanted her anyway and was happy to have her placed in another home. When the LSD Mary had been given began to have its effects, she stops moving her head and legs and sits staring at the wall.

In 1955 and1956, Dr. Bender began hearing glowing accounts about the potential of LSD for producing remarkable results in children suffering mental disorders, including autism and schizophrenia. Bender's earlier work with electroshock therapy had brought her into contact with several other prominent physicians .Dr. Elkes was one of the earliest physicians in Europe to experiment with LSD, having requested samples of the drug from Sandoz Chemical Co. in 1949. Elkes worked closely with the CIA, Pentagon and Britain's MI6 on drug experiments in England and the United States.

Dr. Fink, who was greatly admired by Bender, is considered the godfather of electroshock therapy in the United States. In addition to Fink, Bender also greatly admired the work of Dr. Lothar B. Kalinowsky, a psychiatrist who also consulted closely with the CIA on electroshock matters. Kalinowsky, who was part Jewish and had fled Germany in 1933, was Fink's close friend and, like Fink, was widely recognized as an expert on electroconvulsive therapy. While it is clear from Dr. Bender's papers that she also considered the early LSD work of Dr. Alfred M. Hubbard in Vancouver, Canada, to be very substantial and beneficial, it is important to state here that Hubbard was not a physician nor did he have any formal medical training. Despite the fact that he had no medical credentials and once served time in prison for smuggling, he convinced the Sandoz Chemical Co. into supplying him such ample amounts of LSD. Hubbard's use of LSD in allegedly curing alcoholism is still cited today. How Hubbard so easily passed as a physician is unknown. Even a 1961 paper published by New York Medical College cited Hubbard's LSD work with children, to have been 85% successful.

---

*Two Sisters, LSD and Dr. Buckman*

---

Marion McGill, today an attorney and college professor in the western United States and her sister, Trudy, were sent in 1960 by their parents to be interviewed by Drs. Ling and Buckman at the Chelsea Clinic in London. At the time, Marion was 13 years old and her sister was 15. Marion says that both her mother and father were quite taken with the benefits of LSD and thought that we would also benefit from the drug. Both parents had undergone a series of ten LSD treatments at the Chelsea clinic. While highly successful professionally, their father was a tightly wound, rather angry and insecure man, an accomplished academic, and a narcissist. Their mother was a submissive, obedient, Catholic woman without much identity of her own, other than being a doctor's wife. The sisters were about as normal as any two teenagers could be. They were at the top of their classes in school, had lots of friends, and participated in extracurricular activities. There were to be 10 sessions - once a week for 10 weeks.

The experiences at the clinic where the LSD was administered were quite strange. There was a brief 'interview' by Dr. John Buckman, asking banal questions about health issues, but providing no information about what to expect from the LSD. There was no mention of hallucinations or perceptual distortions or anything frightening. During the 10 sessions, each of which involved an injection, the sisters were kept in separate bedrooms, usually with someone present in the room. There was no effort to counsel the sisters during or after each of these sessions. There was no explanation of what was happening or why it was being done. Most children who are victims of parental abuse do not know how to resist. They fear rejection by parents more than they fear the abuse. The power differential is huge between parents and children and the dependence on parents is virtually absolute. Although each individual session was often terrifying, any lasting effects of the LSD unfolded gradually. In the weeks immediately following the final session, they experienced frequent nightmares such as visions of crawling insects, horrible masks, etc. They couldn't sleep.

Two years after these experiments, during her freshman year in college, one sister suffered a nervous breakdown. The extent to which the LSD may have precipitated this was not known. She had been asking questions about the LSD at this time. The sisters talked about it together, but was afraid to confront their parents. The angrier Marion's sister became, the more she was 'diagnosed' as a 'psychiatric' case and the more medication she was given. To this day, Marion's sister is heavily medicated. She never fully recovered.

Their parents responded to Marion's sister's anger in a way that frightened Marion further. Marion also felt tremendous guilt for not being able to prevent the horrors that her sister endured. Once she was 'classified' as a psychiatric patient, she was lost. Everything that was done to her in the name of 'treatment' seemed to me to be a form of ongoing abuse and torture. The fact that the father was a prominent, internationally known and widely respected physician - and his brother, who had introduced us to this LSD horror, was a prominent, internationally known and widely respected psychiatrist made it impossible to expose them or go against them. Their reputations were more important to them than the health and wellbeing of their daughters. Marion's response was simply to leave home. She never trusted her parents again after the London LSD experience. Marion discovered many other ways in which her father lied, covered up, dissembled and eventually threatened Marion, in order to keep this story from being told.

At the age of 91, the father finally admitted that it had perhaps not been a very good idea to subject the sisters to LSD. The Nazi Doctors who were able to ignore their Hippocratic Oath to 'first, do no harm,' and to inflict unimaginable horrors on their fellow human beings. The loss of Marion sister has been a lifelong source of sorrow for her. Marion attributed it to the LSD and its cover up, whether the chemicals themselves caused her disintegration or not.

*Dr. Bender's Further LSD Experiments on Children*

In 1960, Dr. Bender launched her first experiments with LSD and children. They were conducted within the Children's Unit, Creedmoor State Hospital in Queens, New York. The LSD she used was supplied by Sandoz Pharmaceutical Company. Her initial group of young subjects consisted of 14 children diagnosed schizophrenic, all under the age of 11. There were 11 boys and three girls, ranging in age from six to ten years old.

Jean Marie is almost seven years old. She came here nearly a year ago after her parents abandoned her to the care of an aunt who had no interest in raising her. Marie, who prefers to be called Jean, is shy, withdrawn, and distrustful of most adults she encounters. There are reports she may have been sexually molested by her uncle. Despite her withdrawn nature she smiles easily, and enjoys the company of other children. After receiving LSD on three occasions earlier this month, Marie ceased smiling at all and lost any interest in others her age. In the past week, she seems to have become easily agitated and has lost any interest in reading, something she seemed to very much enjoy before treatment.

In a published report on her 196 LSD experiments with 14 autistic schizophrenic children, Bender states she initially gave each of the children 25 mcg. Of LSD intramuscularly while under continuous observation. She writes: The two oldest boys, over ten years, near or in early puberty, reacted with disturbed anxious behavior. The oldest and most disturbed received Amytal sodium 150 mg. intramuscularly and returned to his usual behavior. Both boys were then excluded from the experiment.

The 12 remaining children were then given injections of 25 mcg. or LSD and then days later were each given 100 mcg. of LSD once a week. Bender's report states: Then it was increased gradually to twice and three times a week as no untoward side-effects were noticed. Finally, it was given daily and this continued for six weeks until the time of this report.

Bender's findings and conclusions concerning her LSD experiments indicated she found the use of the drug promising. Bender reported: In general, the children, were happier; their mood was high in the hours following the ingestion of the drug and they have become more spontaneously playful with balls and balloons. Bender concluded: The use of these drugs will give us more knowledge about both the basic schizophrenic process and the defensive autism in children. Hopefully these drugs will also contribute to our efforts to find better therapeutic agents for early childhood schizophrenia.

In an article published in 1970, Dr. Bender reported on the results of LSD dosing upon two adolescent boys who were mildly schizophrenic. She reported that the boys experienced perceptual distortions. They thought the researchers were making faces at them that their pencils were becoming rubbery, and one boy reported the other boy's face had turned green. The boys began to complain that they were being experimented upon. Even so, Bender and her associate continued the two male adolescents on a regimen of 150 mcg. per day, in divided doses, of LSD. While one of the boys supposedly benefited very much, Bender reported that he later returned to the hospital as a disturbed adult schizophrenic. The other boy kept complaining that he was being experimented upon and they stopped giving him LSD, not because of the drug's effects itself, Bender explained, but because of the boy's attitude towards it.

Dr. Bender's LSD experiments continued into the late 1960s and, during that time, continued to include multiple experiments on children with UML-401, a little known LSD-type drug provided to her by the Sandoz Company, as well as UML-491, also a Sandoz product. Bender's reports on her LSD experiments give no indication of whether the parents or legal guardians of the subject children were aware of, or consented to, the experiments. Over the years, there have been multiple reports that many of Bender's subject children were orphans, but the available literature on the experiments reveals nothing on this. The same literature makes it obvious that the children had been confined to the Creedmoor State Hospital for long periods of time and that many needed suitable homes .There is also no evidence that any follow-up studies were conducted on any of the children experimented upon by Dr. Bender. Today, Dr. Bender is best known and highly regarded in some circles as the creator of the Bender-Gestalt Test, which measures motor skills in children. On Bender's use of LSD on children, Dr. Leon Eisenberg said years later: She did all sorts of things. Lauretta Bender reached success in her career long before randomized controlled trials had even been heard of. She didn't see the need for trials of drugs because she was convinced she knew what worked. Many other physicians speaking privately were far less diplomatic in condemning Bender's LSD work, but, still today, many are reluctant to criticize her continue to cite her work with children as groundbreaking science.

One can easily come to any and all these conclusions simply by reading the professional papers of such scientists and researchers. Not once do any of these papers express concern for the subjects at hand or denote any pangs of conscience at violating any oaths, codes and statutes regarding patient rights, human rights or human dignity. That America's most shameful period of human experimentation, the years 1950 through to about 1979, came on the heels of the making and adoption of the Nuremberg Codes only adds to the shame and hypocrisy. Today, human experimentation is still aggressively conducted by US government-sponsored and employed physicians and scientists regardless of those codes, which came directly out of the shocking madness of the Nazi era. That government-sponsored experimentation still occurs makes a mockery of any governmental efforts, however valid, to protect people from science and a nation that uses its young, its children, for such pursuits is a nation whose commitment to human rights and democratic principles should be seriously questioned and challenged.

## 33.0 Lottery Ticket

If you won the lottery what would you do? Would you share with friends and family or donate to charity. These folks nabbed their 15 minutes of fame and–if they played it smart–the chance to never have to worry about money again. Here's what they said they planned to do with the money:

Merle and Patricia Butler of Red Bud, Illinois and three teachers calling themselves The Three Amigos in Milford Mill, Maryland, as well as an anonymous winner in Ottawa, Kansas, shared the $656 Mega Millions jackpot March 30. That's $218.6 million each. Merle and Patricia Butler were the only winners to come forward publicly, and they were coy about how they planned to spend the money, saying only that they'd take the lump sum of $157 million and spend on the advice of their financial planners and attorneys. What savvy folks. Patricia did tell one media outlet that the couple would do some real good with at least part of their dough. Doubtless everyone in their town of 3,700 would notice if they built a backyard sauna or turned their home into a McMansion.

Eddie Nabors of Dalton, Georgia, and Elaine and Harold Messner of Woodbine, New Jersey, shared Mega Millions on March 6, 2007: $390 million. Nabors, a 52-year-old truck driver, told the Today Show that he planned to buy a house for his daughter so that she could move out of her mobile home, pay off mortgages for his mom, sister, and other family members, and buy a fishing boat for his son. For himself, he reported fairly low-key plans..... fishing.

Jim and Carolyn McCullar, of Ephrata, Washington, won Mega Millions on Jan. 4, 2011 for a total of $380 million. Jim McCullar told reporters that he planned to put his lottery winnings in the bank, write some checks to his six kids, and donate to charity. I'm not going to fly all over the world and buy my own jet, McCullar said in a press conference. What this means to me is the legacy is going to go generation after generation after generation.

Holly Lahti, of Rathdrum, Idaho, won Mega Millions on Jan. 4, 2011: $380 million. Lahti, a single mother, reportedly quit her job as a customer service representative at a bank–and then practically went into hiding. But her estranged husband, Josh Lahti, wasn't shy about sharing his opinion on his wife's winnings. That's awesome! I won't have to pay child support! He told the Associated Press when a reporter informed him of his wife's good fortune. Turns out Holly had good reason to hide: reporters did some digging and found out that the couple was never legally divorced, or even separated, giving Josh a potential, if tenuous, legal claim on Holly's lucky ticket.

Eight workers from a ConAgra meatpacking plant in Nebraska, won Powerball on Feb. 18, 2006, and shared the winnings: $365 million. Seven men and one woman, whose jobs it was to process hams and corned beef, split the winnings. Three immediately quit their jobs, the Today Show reported. Others, after learning they were now millionaires, reported straight to work for the graveyard shift. Two of the winners were immigrants from Vietnam, one from the Congo. Alain Maboussou, the Congolese immigrant, said he planned to use the money to get a business degree. When the lone female winner was asked if she was married, she responded "No. It's all mine".

While our lists might be different, we all have one, don't we? We've all dreamt of what we'd buy or do if we had sudden, overwhelming riches. We certainly wouldn't squander it like the lottery burnouts we've profiled for this article.

Or would we? According to a study published by the University of Kentucky in conjunction with the University of Pittsburgh and Vanderbilt University Law School, lottery winners declare bankruptcy at twice the rate of the general population. Why is this? The inability to squirrel away an unexpected windfall appears to be rooted deep in the human psyche. Money arriving by luck or circumstance is simply easier to spend than money earned through hard work. It's like finding a $20 bill on the sidewalk and splurging at your favorite coffee shop. The researchers also found that lottery winners tended to have below-average education and income, which might translate into lower financial literacy than the average not-that-financially-savvy person. Here are profiles of 10 lottery winners who won big and fell hard.

In 2003, Callie Rogers was 16, living with foster parents in the U.K. and working as a shop clerk earning $5.83 an hour bought a lottery ticket. Rogers won a whopping $3 million in the National Lottery and, despite early insistence that she would continue to live frugally, bought four large homes, several new cars and had two breast augmentations. The suddenly wealthy teenager also developed a penchant for sharing her windfall with others. She purchased expensive gifts for a series of boyfriends. She even bought one boyfriend a car and paid him to act as her chauffer because at 16, she was too young to drive. It was another habit, however, that really led to Rogers's financial ruin: cocaine. She estimates spending a quarter of a million pounds on the drug. After the dust settled, Rogers was left with little to show for her riches. She sold the homes she owned, divested the new cars and rented a modest townhouse, saving the seemingly paltry $64,000 that remained of her winnings while picking up work as a maid. However, in April 2012, low on funds, pregnant with twins and with a new loving boyfriend at her side, Rogers said, For the first time I feel like I have everything I need. Sadly, one of the twins died shortly after birth

In 2002, Michael Carroll won the U.K.'s National Lottery, netting a $15.8 million boost for his bank account. By 2012, however, the former garbage collector was living on public benefits, having squandered the money in myriad ways. Carroll purchased -- and then destroyed -- a mansion, threw lavish parties for friends and made a daily habit of smoking $3,000 worth of crack cocaine. He also bought pricey cars, wrecked them on the self-made race track circling the grounds of his mansion and then left them to rust on the property's outskirts. A fair amount of his lotto payment went to prostitutes and overstated gold jewelry, and he developed a penchant for drinking alcohol and then driving around the otherwise quiet streets of Norfolk, England. The disturbances occurred on such a predictable basis, a hotline was established so neighbors could report Carroll to the local council. Eventually, financial shortfalls forced Carroll to sell the mansion at a loss and he was later caught leaving a grocery market without paying for the sandwich and drink he grabbed off store shelves. The $17 items ended up costing him nearly $138 in court costs.

From an early age, William Bud Post's life had not been easy. His mother died when he was 8 and his father sent him to an orphanage. From there, he became a carnival worker and held down a series of odd jobs with meager pay that didn't afford certain luxuries -- like home- or car-ownership. But that all changed when in 1998, with less than $3 in his checking account, Post pawned a ring for $40 and spent the proceeds on Pennsylvania Lottery tickets. When he walked away with a $16.2 million jackpot, it seemed as though his luck had changed. Not so fast. Once word of his good fortune spread, his landlady (and sometime girlfriend) demanded and received one-third of the winnings, claiming he'd promised to split the winnings with her after she bought the tickets for him. His brother hired a killer to take Post's life, but only after Post purchased businesses and cars for him and his siblings. Post also made some questionable financial decisions, like buying an airplane he could not fly and a mansion that was eventually sold for parts to erase his mounting debts. To clear other debts, Post sold the rights to his remaining lottery payments, but ended up spending his last $2.65 million on two homes, several motorcycles, three cars, a truck and a sailboat, among other things. He racked up seven marriages, too. I was much happier when I was broke, said Sullivan. And just when circumstances didn't seem like they could get worse, they did. Years earlier, in those first, heady months of being a rich man, Post had fired a gun at a bill collector and was charged with assault. Nearly penniless, the lottery winner eventually served the sentence and then lived on a $450 disability payment until he died at age 66, eight years after winning big.

Jack Whittaker lost more than half a million dollars at a strip club. You'd have thought this one wouldn't have ended so badly. When Jack Whittaker won $315 million playing Powerball in 2002 -- the largest single jackpot at the time as he was already a millionaire, so he knew how to handle money. He'd spent decades building a successful water and sewer pipeline company in West Virginia worth a reported $17 million and already lavished clothes and gifts on his wife and granddaughter Brandi Bragg, who lived with them part-time. But winning the lottery gave him something entrepreneurial wealth never did: fame. And that, Whittaker later said, was more than he and his family could handle. He volleyed continual requests for money and endured the public airing of his strip club, gambling and drinking habits. His wife of nearly 42 years divorced him. And then there were the thieves. They stole Whittaker's briefcase containing $545,000 from the strip club, and in another incident, stole $100,000 that Whittaker had left in plain sight on the passenger seat of his car. Some of his employees also embezzled funds. Although Whittaker set up a foundation that constructed churches, funded college scholarships and donated to those in need, trouble plagued his own family. His beloved Brandi had been only 15 when Whittaker won the lottery. By 17, she was dead, her body found wrapped in tarp behind a junked van. An autopsy revealed recent cocaine use. Not long after, Whittaker's daughter and Brandi's mother, who suffered from recurring lymphoma, was also found dead.

Lisa Arcand's dream business of a seafood restaurant closed six months after it opened. In April 2004, Lisa Arcand was a single mother living in Lawrence, Mass., when she bought a lottery ticket. Within days, her purchase paid off: She'd become a millionaire. And like many newly minted millionaires, Arcand starting splurging immediately. First, she hosted a party for 20 of her friends and family, who ordered several $200 bottles of wine during the bash. She enrolled her son in a private school with $10,000 annual tuition, went on a couple of vacations, and bought a house filled with new furniture. Then she embarked on her dream of buying and operating a hometown restaurant. However, fewer than six months after opening the seafood restaurant, financial woes forced Arcand to shutter the eatery. Of all the new things Arcand tried, the one thing she didn't do was save a nest egg. I talked to a few people, but determined that putting money away wasn't worth it, she said. While the lottery mandated annual payments of $35,000 rather than a lump sum, a financial services company aggressively went after her, offering an upfront payment of $200,000 in exchange for $15,000 per year of her winnings. While this gave her more up-front cash, it put her in a higher tax bracket, further reducing her money. Left with a failed business, an empty savings account and few prospects on the horizon until she received her next annual lottery payment, Arcand was resigned to wait for her luck to turn. Again.

Even though Janite Lee gave thousands to charity, the lotto gods did not smile on her. She eventually declared bankruptcy after too much spending. Lottery winner Janite Lee seemed to have the right idea. In 1993, after buying a lottery ticket worth $18 million, the 52-year-old South Korean immigrant gave much of the spoils to charity. Although Lee did move into a million-dollar house in St. Louis, the city where she'd previously operated a wig shop, she focused on helping others. With $620,000 a year winnings, Lee's charitable efforts included sizable donations to Washington University School of Law. She also donated hundreds of thousands to presidential political campaigns, which earned her tableside seating with Bill Clinton and Al Gore. Unfortunately, while she was giving away her lottery earnings, Lee was protecting a financial secret. Remember that million-dollar house? Instead of buying it with her lottery windfall, Lee purchased it on payments. In addition to this mortgage, she leased luxury cars and reportedly borrowed millions more from banks and credit cards. Even when she tried to make financially savvy moves, such as paying off a loan ahead of schedule, she ended up deeper in debt by owing $750,000 in early payoff penalties. By 2001, Lee had sold the rights to future lottery payments and filed for bankruptcy. She was $2.5 million in debt.

## 34.0 Cannibalism

Could you be cannibalistic? Do you have to be sick minded? Indulging in the flesh on purpose. What if it were to survive? Would you wait until they died before dining or would you be able to kill them? Perhaps maybe you would be the one to offer to die to save the rest. When it comes to surviving do you really know what you would do? Stories have been told of those stranded in the ocean or in the mountains and the survivors had to consume their travel mates or friends. I could not spend the rest of my days wondering where my actions may send me.

# Poetry

*Ω*

***If there were such a power***

***It would be to see your soul***

***To read the mind of a lover***

***Validate what you already know***

***Heal them with your compassion***

***Cure them with infinite dedication***

***Remove all material lusts***

***Show them what lies beneath***

***Hand them your beating heart***

***God knows I would hand you the universe***

***If you handed me your heart***

***I would make the moon glow for you***

***For just one midnight kiss***

Ω

***Inspiration lies in life itself***

***A story told by all things relevant***

***A feeling shown by all you know***

***Poetry is not about the author***

***Poetry is the author showing life***

***Things in words***

***Others cannot speak***

Ω

***If you risk it all to touch their soul***

***Ensure they return the favor***

*Ω*

***When flaws become perfection***

***Then you have found love***

*Ω*

***Conversations***

***Talks that only we could make***

***My imagination bursting wide open***

***Sharing something deep inside***

***Secrets revealed like never before***

***How you broke the lock***

***I will never be sure***

***My favorite dreams***

***Washed closer to shore***

*Drifting to sleep easier than before*

*You made it all go away*

*All the pain and all the hurt*

*Just for a moment*

*I was free of tears*

*Free from my own tainted soul*

*Then came the silence*

*When you walked away*

*And took all the shards of me*

*Ω*

*I Can't Give You*

*My soul begs to give to you*

*What my brain and body cannot*

***Damaged goods you have collected***

***Nothing can be corrected***

***Lacking empathy; Lacking intimacy***

***My words are all that I can offer***

***For my actions do suffer***

***All that has been; All that could be***

***I can only hope***

***When ink meets paper***

***Smooth lines of written despair***

***Hidden joys in curves of letters***

***A tear in a consonant***

***A laugh in a vowel***

***Actions in play***

***Actions in reality***

***This I do fear***

***Ω***

## ***Send Me There***

***Send me away to place all my own***

***Let me write until my mind runs dry***

***Supply me with paper and ink***

***Let my hands do the work***

***Til' there is work no more***

***Let words spill from my lips like song***

***Words be inked and pass them along***

***If they are not worthy now***

***Let have meaning when I am gone***

***Let me inspire***

***Let me comfort***

***Let me write what I cannot show***

***For I only want to touch just one soul***

***Beyond the oceans rim***

***Let my words console your sin***

*Ω*

***I now crave***

***The thing I once feared the most***

***Solitude***

***Now I lay with relief***

***Alone with my own peace***

***A chance to let my mind wander***

***My soul a moment to drift***

*Changes from the usual chaos*

*Like waves upon the sea*

*My thoughts are scattered*

*Skipping tracks like a scratched record*

*The needle playing in random order*

*Inspiration comes and thrives*

*The one moment of blissful dullness*

*Another wave splashes my mind*

*Scattering the sands of sanity*

*I now crave*

*The thing I feared the most*

*Solitude*

*Ω*

***Because of you***

***I changed how I thought***

***Changed how I felt***

***Kept inside what should've been said***

***Smothered feelings I should've shown***

***Withheld actions that proved my heart***

***All that I was; All that you loved***

***Twisted and changed***

***Now I show no self***

***You ask why I'm withheld***

***You created this mess***

***A box locked away***

***Is my true self***

Ω

*I know now*

*I do not belong in this realm*

*Waves within me*

*Crashing upon rocky shores*

*Like a tattered soul*

*Ripped to shreds by thine self*

*But as I swim; Fighting*

*I think of you*

*For I know*

*Even though the words unspoken*

*You think of me*

*You miss my smile*

*Knowing the love that remains a whisper*

***Calms the waves***

***To gentle ripples***

***Glinting beautiful moon***

***As I take my last drowning breath***

***It will be your name upon my lips***

*Ω*

***Dying Soul***

***I can smell your sickness***

***Slow decay inside***

***Rotting thoughts of a dying soul***

***Panic and fear of where she will go***

***When I think I'm done***

***There is more to come***

***Words that flow***

***Like putrid bile from deep below.***

Ω

***Crazy***

***Crazy Is***

***Crazy does***

***From which inspiration doth come***

***Intense joy***

***Devotion misplaced***

***Souls encased***

***A rambling mind***

***Of emotions entwined***

# Quotes

*"Every man dies. Not every man really lives."-Williams Wallace.*

*"I arise ton between a desire to improve the world and a desire to enjoy the world. This makes it hard to plan the day." – E.B. White.*

*"Certainly, travel the seeing of sights: it is a change that goes on, deep and permanent, in the ideas of living."-Anonymous*

*"You are never too old to see another goal or to dream a new dream."- C.S. Lewis*

*"The best, most beautiful things in the world cannot be seen or even touched; they must be felt with the heart." -Helen Keller*

*"There is no heavier burden than having too many desires." -Anonymous*

*"Education is a progressive discovery of our own ignorance." -Anonymous*

*"I don't believe you have to be better than everybody else. I believe you have to be better than you ever thought you could be."- Ken Venturi*

*"An eye for an eye ends up making the whole world blind."- Mahatma Gandhi*

*"I've learned that people will forget what you said, people will forget what you did, but people will never forget how you made them feel."- Maya Angelou*

*"You must be the change you wish to see in the world."– Gandhi*

*"The traveler sees what he sees, the tourist see what he has come to see". -Anonymous*

*"The world is a book, and those who do not travel read only a page." - Saint Augustine*

*"I'd rather regret the things I've done than regret the things I haven't done."-Lucille Ball*

*"The greatest Power is often simple patience." - Anonymous*

*"Good people do not need laws to tell them to act responsibly, while bad people will find a way around the laws."–Plato*

*"Never be bullied into silence. Never allow yourself to be made a victim. Accept no one's definition of your life. Define yourself." -Anonymous*

*"How vain is it to sit down to write when you have not stood up to live." – Henry David Thoreau*

*"Do not confine your children to your own learning, for they were born in another time". - Chinese Proverb*

*"Satisfaction of one's curiosity is one of the greatest sources of happiness in life." -Anonymous*

*"Happiness is found in doing, not merely possessing"- napoleon*

*"It is not length of life, but depth of life".-Ralph Waldo Emerson*

*"Hope is the thing with feathers; that perches in the soul*

*And sings the tune without the words; and never stops at all." — Emily Dickinson*

*"If I can stop one heart from breaking, I shall not live in vain." — Emily Dickinson*

*"That it will never come again is what makes life so sweet." — Emily Dickinson*

*"If I read a book and it makes my whole body so cold no fire can ever warm me, I know that is poetry."— Emily Dickinson*

*"Not knowing when the dawn will come; I open every door." — Emily Dickinson*

*"Morning without you is a dwindled dawn." — Emily Dickinson*

*"Forever is composed of nows." — Emily Dickinson*

*"Saying nothing sometimes says the most." — Emily Dickinson*

*"This is my letter to the world; that never wrote to me" — Emily Dickinson*

*"I dwell in possibility…" — Emily Dickinson*

*"To live is so startling it leaves little time for anything else." — Emily Dickinson*

*"I'm nobody! Who are you?*

*Are you – Nobody – too?*

*Then there's a pair of us?*

*Don't tell! They'd advertise – you know!*

*How dreary – to be – Somebody!*

*How public – like a Frog*

*To tell one's name – the livelong June*

*To an admiring Bog!" — Emily Dickinson*

*"Dogs are better than human beings because they know but do not tell." — Emily Dickinson*

*"Pardon My Sanity in a World Insane" — Emily Dickinson*

*"A word is dead when it's been said, some say. I say it just begins to live that day." — Emily Dickinson*

*"The soul should always stand ajar, ready to welcome the ecstatic experience." — Emily Dickinson*

*"How happy is the little stone*

*That rambles in the road alone,*

*And doesn't care about careers,*

*And exigencies never fears;*

*Whose coat of elemental brown*

*A passing universe put on;*

*And independent as the sun,*

*Associates or glows alone,*

*Fulfilling absolute decree*

*In casual simplicity." — Emily Dickinson*

*"There is no Frigate like a book*

*To take us Lands away,*

*Nor any Coursers like a Page*

*Of prancing Poetry..." — Emily Dickinson*

*"Truth is so rare; it is delightful to tell it." — Emily Dickinson*

*"The dearest ones of time, the strongest friends of the soul--BOOKS." — Emily Dickinson*

*"Hold dear to your parents for it is a scary and confusing world without them." — Emily Dickinson*

*"We turn not older with years but newer every day." — Emily Dickinson*

*"Life is a spell so exquisite that everything conspires to break it." — Emily Dickinson*

*"I felt it shelter to speak to you." — Emily Dickinson*

*"The Heart wants what it wants - or else it does not care" — Emily Dickinson*

*"But a Book is only the Heart's Portrait- every Page a Pulse." — Emily Dickinson*

*"How do most people live without any thought? There are many people in the world,--you must have noticed them in the street,--and how do they live? How do they get strength to put on their clothes in the morning?" — Emily Dickinson*

*"A wounded dear leaps the highest" — Emily Dickinson*

*"Write me of hope and love, and hearts that endured." — Emily Dickinson*

*"They say that God is everywhere and yet we always think of him as somewhat of a recluse." — Emily Dickinson*

*"Dying is a wild night and a new road." — Emily Dickinson*

*"The brain is wider than the sky,*

*For, put them side by side,*

*The one the other will include*

*With ease and you beside." — Emily Dickinson*

*"That love is all there is, is all we know of love." — Emily Dickinson*

*"People need hard times and oppression to develop psychic muscles." — Emily Dickinson*

*"My best Acquaintances are those; With Whom I spoke no Word" — Emily Dickinson*

*"I am nobody! Who are you? Are you a nobody, too?" — Emily Dickinson*

*“Luck is not chance, it's toil; fortune's expensive smile is earned.” — Emily Dickinson*

*“I only achieve simplicity with enormous effort. -Clarice Lispector*

*“A woman must have money and a room of her own if she is to write fiction."- Virginia Woolf*

*“The first draft of anything is shit. -Ernest Hemingway*

*“Always be a poet, even in prose. -Charles Baudelaire*

*“If you do not breathe through writing, if you do not cry out in writing, or sing in writing, then don’t write, because our culture has no use for it. -Anaïs Nin*

*“One can be absolutely truthful and sincere even though admittedly the most outrageous liar. Fiction and invention are of the very fabric of life. -Henry Miller*

*“Writers aren’t people exactly. Or, if they’re any good, they’re a whole lot of people trying so hard to be one person. -F. Scott Fitzgerald*

*“The true writer has nothing to say. What counts is the way he says it. Alain Robbe-Grillet*

*“Life is painful and disappointing. It is useless, therefore, to write new realistic novels. We generally know where we stand in relation to reality and don’t care to know any more."- Michel Houellebecq*

*“Do you realize that all great literature is all about what a bummer it is to be a human being? Isn’t it such a relief to have somebody say that?"- Kurt Vonnegut*

*"Don't bend; don't water it down; don't try to make it logical; don't edit your own soul according to the fashion. Rather, follow your most intense obsessions mercilessly. Franz Kafka*

*"Reading is more important than writing."- Roberto Bolaño*

*"The artist is always beginning. Any work of art which is not a beginning, an invention, a discovery is of little worth."- Ezra Pound*

*"The person born with a talent they are meant to use will find their greatest happiness in using it. -Johann Wolfgang von Goethe*

*"We live not only in a world of thoughts, but also in a world of things. Words without experience are meaningless. -Vladimir Nabokov*

*"Describe your sorrows and desires, the thoughts that pass through your mind and your belief in some kind of beauty – describe all these with heartfelt, silent, humble sincerity and, when you express to be alive—is Power." — Emily Dickinson*

*"To hope means to be ready at every moment for that which is not yet born, and yet not become desperate if there is no birth in our lifetime." — Emily Dickinson*

*"Opinion is a fitting thing but truth outlasts the sun - if then we cannot own them both, possess the oldest one." — Emily Dickinson*

*"I lost a world the other day. Has anybody found? You'll know it by the rows of stars around its forehead bound. A rich man might not notice it; yet to my frugal*

*eye of more esteem than ducats. Oh! Find it, sir, for me!" — Emily Dickinson*

*"Old age comes on suddenly, and not gradually as is thought." — Emily Dickinson*

*"The poet lights the light and fades away. But the light goes on and on." — Emily Dickinson*

*"The truth I do not dare to know I muffle with a jest." — Emily Dickinson*

*"There is no greater agony than bearing an untold story inside you." — Maya Angelou*

*"You have to write the book that wants to be written. And if the book will be too difficult for grown-ups, then you write it for children." — Madeleine L'Engle*

*"There is nothing to writing. All you do is sit down at a typewriter and bleed." — Ernest Hemingway*

*"What really knocks me out is a book that, when you're all done reading it, you wish the author that wrote it was a terrific friend of yours and you could call him up on the phone whenever you felt like it. That doesn't happen much, though." — J.D. Salinger, The Catcher in the Rye*

*"If there's a book that you want to read, but it hasn't been written yet, then you must write it." — Toni Morrison*

*"If you don't have time to read, you don't have the time (or the tools) to write. Simple as that." — Stephen King*

*"Lock up your libraries if you like; but there is no gate, no lock, and no bolt that you can set upon the freedom of my mind." — Virginia Woolf*

*"Substitute 'damn' every time you're inclined to write 'very;' your editor will delete it and the writing will be just as it should be." — Mark Twain*

*"You never have to change anything you got up in the middle of the night to write." — Saul Bellow*

*"The difference between the right word and the almost right word is the difference between lightning and a lightning bug." — Mark Twain*

*"Fantasy is hardly an escape from reality. It's a way of understanding it." — Lloyd Alexander*

*"One day I will find the right words, and they will be simple." — Jack Kerouac*

*"And by the way, everything in life is writable about if you have the outgoing guts to do it, and the imagination to improvise. The worst enemy to creativity is self-doubt." — Sylvia Plath, The Unabridged Journals of Sylvia Plath*

*"No tears in the writer, no tears in the reader. No surprise in the writer, no surprise in the reader." — Robert Frost*

*"You must stay drunk on writing so reality cannot destroy you." — Ray Bradbury, Zen in the Art of Writing*

*"Read, read, and read. Read everything -- trash, classics, good and bad, and see how they do it. Just*

*like a carpenter who works as an apprentice and studies the master. Read! You'll absorb it.Then write. If it's good, you'll find out. If it's not, throw it out of the window." — William Faulkner*

*"Fiction is the truth inside the lie." — Stephen King*

*"Writing is a socially acceptable form of schizophrenia." — E.L. Doctorow*

*"Don't tell me the moon is shining; show me the glint of light on broken glass." — Anton Chekhov*

*"History will be kind to me for I intend to write it." — Winston Churchill*

*"Words can be like X-rays if you use them properly -- they'll go through anything. You read and you're pierced." — Aldous Huxley*

*"How vain it is to sit down to write when you have not stood up to live." — Henry David Thoreau*

*"We have to continually be jumping off cliffs and developing our wings on the way down." — Kurt Vonnegut*

*"Whatever the mind of man can conceive and believe, it can achieve. –Napoleon Hill*

*"Strive not to be a success, but rather to be of value." – Albert Einstein*

*"Two roads diverged in a wood, and I—I took the one less traveled by, and that has made all the difference." –Robert Frost*

*"I attribute my success to this: I never gave or took any excuse. –Florence Nightingale*

*"You miss 100% of the shots you don't take. –Wayne Gretzky*

*"Every strike brings me closer to the next home run."–Babe Ruth*

*"The past is a ghost, the future a dream. All we ever have is now. "–Bill Cosby*

*"Life is what happens to you while you're busy making other plans." –John Lennon*

*"We become what we think about."–Earl Nightingale*

*"Twenty years from now you will be more disappointed by the things that you didn't do than by the ones you did do, so throw off the bowlines, sail away from safe harbor, and catch the trade winds in your sails. Explore, Dream, Discover. "–Mark Twain*

*"The most common way people give up their power is by thinking they don't have any."–Alice Walker*

*"The mind is everything. What you think you become. "–Buddha*

*The best time to plant a tree was 20 years ago. The second best time is now". –Chinese Proverb*

*"An unexamined life is not worth living." –Socrates*

*"Eighty percent of success is showing up." –Woody Allen*

*"Your time is limited, so don't waste it living someone else's life."–Steve Jobs*

*"Winning isn't everything, but wanting to win is." –Vince Lombardi*

*"I am not a product of my circumstances. I am a product of my decisions"–Stephen Covey*

*"Every child is an artist. The problem is how to remain an artist once he grows up." –Pablo Picasso*

*"You can never cross the ocean until you have the courage to lose sight of the shore."–Christopher Columbus*

*"I've learned that people will forget what you said, people will forget what you did, but people will never forget how you made them feel."–Maya Angelou*

*"Either you run the day, or the day runs you. –Jim Rohn*

*"Whether you think you can or you think you can't, you're right."–Henry Ford*

*"The two most important days in your life are the day you are born and the day you find out why." –Mark Twain*

*"Whatever you can do, or dream you can, begin it. Boldness has genius, power and magic in it." –Johann Wolfgang von Goethe*

*"The best revenge is massive success. –Frank Sinatra*

*"There is only one way to avoid criticism: do nothing, say nothing, and be nothing." –Aristotle*

*"The only person you are destined to become is the person you decide to be."–Ralph Waldo Emerson*

*"Go confidently in the direction of your dreams.  Live the life you have imagined." –Henry David Thoreau*

*"How wonderful it is that nobody need wait a single moment before starting to improve the world." –Anne Frank*

*"When I let go of what I am, I become what I might be." –Lao Tzu*

*"Life is not measured by the number of breaths we take, but by the moments that take our breath away. "– Maya Angelou*

*"We must believe that we are gifted for something, and that this thing, at whatever cost, must be attained."– Marie Curie*

*"Too many of us are not living our dreams because we are living our fears."–Les Brown*

*"Challenges are what make life interesting and overcoming them is what makes life meaningful." – Joshua J. Marine*

*"In order to succeed, your desire for success should be greater than your fear of failure". –Bill Cosby*

*"A person who never made a mistake never tried anything new." – Albert Einstein*

*"I would rather die of passion than of boredom." – Vincent van Gogh*

*“A truly rich man is one whose children run into his arms when his hands are empty.”–Unknown*

*“It is not what you do for your children, but what you have taught them to do for themselves, that will make them successful human beings.” –Ann Landers*

*“If you want your children to turn out well, spend twice as much time with them, and half as much money.” –Abigail Van Buren*

*“Do what you can, where you are, with what you have. –Teddy Roosevelt*

*“Dreaming, after all, is a form of planning. “ –Gloria Steinem*

*“You may be disappointed if you fail, but you are doomed if you don’t try. “ –Beverly Sills*

*“Remember no one can make you feel inferior without your consent. “ –Eleanor Roosevelt*

*“Life is what we make it, always has been, always will be. “ –Grandma Moses*

*“The question isn’t who is going to let me; it’s who is going to stop me. “ –Ayn Rand*

*“It’s not the years in your life that count. It’s the life in your years. “–Abraham Lincoln*

# About The Author

Jennifer Johnson is from a small town in Indiana. She is a scuba diver, traveler, small time actress, step-mother of two, and career woman. Jennifer began writing at an early age and the passion has stuck with her since producing serval single and collaborative publications. She has been locally nominated in the "Who's Who" of literary arts, is a member of the local Writer's Guild, and has been nominated in Indiana Emerging Authors. Jennifer's publications can be found on createspace.com, amazon.com, and her local bookstores.

# Reviews

## Reviewed by Mamta Madhavan for Readers' Favorite

## One Mind's Words

One Mind's Words by Jennifer Johnson is a collection of poems about life and life's lessons. The author has interspersed the emotions and the lessons learnt from life in the poems and has managed to bring out a very impressive collection. The poems have some message for all of us out there who have experienced the same emotions but have not really taken the time to think about it.

I enjoyed this collection because every poem has a message which the author has conveyed with elan. Each poem begins with a saying based on the author's lessons in life and observations. The language is simple and elegant and the wordplay is excellent, adding to the effectiveness of the author's thoughts. All the poems that follow the quotes express the views of the quote in a more detailed manner.

One Mind's Words has some inspiring poems which motivate you to change and take a look at yourself. It teaches you how to look at life with all its beauty and flaws. It is difficult to say which poem is good. All the poems have some profound thought in them which can help you change your thinking. These poems can capture the interest of any reader, even if they are not poetry lovers. It is because all the poems are written targeting the common man and the emotions experienced.

### Steven A Williams-Author, Poet

These pieces are written with such vulnerability, honesty, and intimacy, they can't help but to be deeply touching, and create quite a personal introspective look into the writer's life. They are stitched together to tell a sad, inspiring, and hopeful story of love, family, challenge, strength, and triumph. They are also displayed in an original format serving the double purpose of being a child's advice to carry them through all the changes of life which is culminated in "My Child", one of the best pieces in the collection. This writer has an incredibly strong voice throughout her work which is one of the most important building blocks of a great poet!

### Steven A Williams-Author, Poet
### One Mind's Words II

In Jennifer Johnson's sophomore effort here, she displays the same voice, and powerful vulnerability which existed in her first collection but now adds to this one beautiful imagery, metaphors, and wonderful prose! This is shown early on in the poem "Covered Up" which contains the best line in the entire book...Upon these sands of time we don't remember the treasures...other great pieces here include the hopeful and philosophical "Religion", the moving and clever "Inspiration", the romantic and sweet "Pleasure", and the eerie and chilling "Figure in the Door". As can be expected from her, Jennifer Johnson takes you on a contemplative and inspiring journey here, ending in triumph and personal strength which leave the reader wiser for having read it!

### Steven A Williams-Author, Poet
### Random Thoughts

Here is another great collection of poetry and thought by a wonderful independent author. This one far more vulnerable and personal than the last which makes it a pleasure and an introspective journey to read. The first section contains some great philosophy and conversation starting thought reflection, but the second section steals the show! Beautiful, fluid, and in most cases, brilliant poetry showing an amazing level of maturity and evolution from the authors previous work. This book is a wonderful collection and a benefit to any mind and soul to read!

### Kimberly DuBois
### Random Thoughts

This collection is very moving. It is introspective, thoughtful and deeply felt. The author poses deep questions and writes with emotion. She is being genuine and honest in this book, which I enjoyed. A book that makes you think!

## Sophia Frazier

## One Mind's Words II

I read this author's first in the series and enjoyed it. It made sense to read the second book too! I look forward to more from this author.

## Steven A Williams-Author, Poet

## One Mind's Words II

In Jennifer Johnson's sophomore effort here, she displays the same voice, and powerful vulnerability which existed in her first collection but now adds to this one beautiful imagery, metaphors, and wonderful prose! This is shown early on in the poem "Covered Up" which contains the best line in the entire book...Upon these sands of time we don't remember the treasures...other great pieces here include the hopeful and philosophical "Religion", the moving and clever "Inspiration", the romantic and sweet "Pleasure", and the eerie and chilling "Figure in the Door". As can be expected from her, Jennifer Johnson takes you on a contemplative and inspiring journey here, ending in triumph and personal strength which leave the reader wiser for having read it!

## Steven A Williams-Author, Poet

## Red Eyes

An amazing collection written with raw emotion, and powerful depth! This collection, by now seasoned veteran in independent poetry Jennifer Johnson, is a beautifully, tastefully, artistically, crafted story of dealing with sadness and pain and rising out of it stronger and wiser. The pieces within are intimate, vulnerable, and brave (which has become a staple for this emotional poet) and paint an emotional mental picture for the reader in a sobering way. The poems in this book appear to be ordered in certain groups regarding with specific emotions and mental states which helps carry the reader through the journey with the poet. The book starts out in a rather painful, sorrowful place, then battles with those feelings, unwilling to accept them. Soon, though, the poems begin to deal with these emotions and, over time, the poet gets stronger from the pain and the darkness. What you have at the climactic end to the collection is a wiser, more philosophical poet regarding the world in a deeper way and a stronger person determined to turn pain and hardship into unfettered inspiration. This is a great collection of poetry and holds the power to connect with readers and with the world in a profound way.

## Reviewed by Mamta Madhavan for Readers' Favorite

## One Mind's Words II

One Mind's Words II by Jennifer Johnson is a beautiful collection of poems that reflect on life, emotions, and the changes that happen in our lives. The poems are subtle yet emotional with a lot of depth and underlying messages to the reader. The Life Lesson at the beginning of each poem motivates readers more to handle their lives in a positive manner and it opens one's perspective to a wider plane.

All the poems have some meaning, some message, and much profound advice. The style is simple, appealing, and the use of metaphor is wonderful, making the poems classy and excellent. The poet has done different types of formatting for different poems, making the visual aspect greater. My personal favorite is 'As I Walk' which inspires a person to keep looking out for opportunities in life. 'Paths' is another beautiful poem. It is profound with a message and the imagery is wonderful. There is a lot of beautiful imagery in these poems, enhancing the visual aspect.

The poet also speaks about life's changes and how things alter as we age. The poet touches a relevant topic in her poem 'Nuclear Dream.' Abuse is something that many of us are subjected to and the author tells us to prevent abuse and save others and oneself from it. Overall, I was impressed by this collection. It is something that any of us can relate to and understand. I look forward to reading her next collection

*Reviewed by Mamta Madhavan for Readers' Favorite*

## Our Journey

Our Journey by Jennifer Johnson, Hailey Johnson, and Jericha Johnson is a beautiful collection of poems based on relationships and family bonding, particularly between a step-mother and her step-daughters. It is about a family's growth and progress in their personal relationships. And it can be applied to all the relationships. I enjoyed all the poems in the book. The theme of relationships appears in all the poems and most of the poems make you feel that they are semi-confessional. The bonding between step-parents and step-children is explained. The poems are motivational and inspiring. The poets manage to express all the emotions. The language is simple and the poems are worded very well. They capture the essence of what the poets actually want to convey to the reader. My personal favorite in this would be 'Goodbye Child' where a mother speaks about how her child has left her childhood and youth and is beginning a new adult life. It is a feeling experienced by all parents, especially mothers when their daughters grow up. This collection is penned by three poets. All speak of family and bonding, the love shared between them. A few have sad emotions but they end on some positive notes, giving a feeling of hope to the reader. It's good to read poems penned by different poets in the same book. Similar emotions will be interpreted in different ways to the reader.

# If you enjoyed this; try this:

- ✓ Random Thoughts
- ✓ One Mind's Words
- ✓ One Mind's Words II
- ✓ Our Journey
- ✓ Red Eyes

Made in the USA
Coppell, TX
20 October 2026

93449776R00135